SUPERSONIC

SUPE

RSONIC

The Design and Lifestyle of Concorde

© Prestel Verlag, Munich • London • New York 2018
A member of Verlagsgruppe Random House GmbH
Neumarkter Strasse 28 • 81673 Munich

Prestel Publishing Ltd.
14-17 Wells Street
London W1T 3PD

Prestel Publishing
900 Broadway, Suite 603
New York, NY 10003

Library of Congress Cataloging-in-Publication Data

Names: Azerrad, Lawrence, author.
Title: Supersonic : the design and lifestyle of Concorde / by Lawrence
    Azerrad ; foreword by Sir Terence Conran ; afterword by Cindy Crawford and
    Andrew Macpherson.
Description: Munich ; New York : Prestel, 2018.
Identifiers: LCCN 2018007153 | ISBN 9783791384092 (hardback)
Subjects: LCSH: Concorde (Jet transports) | BISAC: TRANSPORTATION / Aviation
    / History. | TRANSPORTATION / Aviation / General. | DESIGN / Industrial.
Classification: LCC TL685.7 .A99 2018 | DDC 629.133/349--dc23
LC record available at https://lccn.loc.gov/2018007153

A CIP catalogue record for this book is available from the British Library.

Editorial Direction: Holly La Due
Copyediting: Kara Pickman
Proofreading: Susan Richmond
Production: Luke Chase
Design: Lawrence Azerrad and Frankie Hamersma for LADdesign Inc.

Typeset in DINPro and Chalet Paris Nineteen Eighty

MIX
Paper from
responsible sources
FSC® C008047

Verlagsgruppe Random House FSC® N001967

Printed in China

ISBN 978-3-7913-8409-2

www.prestel.com

SUPERSONIC

The Design and Lifestyle of Concorde

Lawrence Azerrad

Foreword by Sir Terence Conran

Afterword by Cindy Crawford and Andrew Macpherson

PRESTEL

Munich · London · New York

Original interior design of British Airways Concorde cabin, 1974

French postcard showing preproduction Concorde, 1976

TABLE OF CONTENTS

Sir Terence Conran with actor
Nigel Havers and his wife
Polly Havers on Concorde,
October 24, 2003

FOREWORD

Sir Terence Conran

Concorde is the most iconic aircraft of all time and I can honestly say that it is the most beautiful and exhilarating man-made object I have ever seen. It is one of the few designs to take my breath away. It had that magic ingredient of the truly special and it inspired the imagination of millions of people all over the world.

It was instantly recognizable, immediately eye-catching, unspeakably elegant and so it became one of the great design icons of the modern age.

Watching Concorde fly was to witness that rare, dynamic combination of graceful elegance with the raw energy and power of supersonic flight. Flying on Concorde was something different altogether though—that terrific, exhilarating surge, the blast of power, and then the momentary feeling that you had left your stomach behind in the terminal.

Concorde arrived in a relatively gloomy period in the twentieth century and immediately became a global symbol of luxury, glamour, ambition, and human achievement. In a heartbeat it raised the spirit and opened our eyes to something that had never been experienced before—supersonic travel. Just the very idea was utterly seductive.

Concorde was a head turner, so far ahead of its time that when it made its first speed-defying passenger flight across the Atlantic in 1976 it gave us all an irresistible glimpse into the future, captivating us instantly and daring us to dream. It remains as thrilling today as it was when it first pushed out of the aerodrome in Filton, England.

I have always felt that by very definition, planes are beautiful objects because their functionality requires a graceful solution and Concorde was the most stunning of all. It became *the* aircraft of the twentieth century. It combined exquisite beauty and form with enormous engineering invention and excellence. It was an unparalleled recipe of art, design, science, engineering, and bold imaginative thinking.

From the first moment I heard about the project, it captured my imagination. It wasn't just me; the jet inspired millions of people around the world. It became the embodiment of thoughtful, forward-thinking design.

The key to Concorde's success was developing the technology to make the ideas a reality and bringing this most fantastic of dreams to life. Working side by side, the British and French engineers overcame every obstacle and the project became a great melting pot of ideas and technical advances—it was *the* great moment for European aviation. To work on the project must have been a dream come true.

Do not think I exaggerate when I say that Concorde is the single most important piece of design in my long lifetime. Will we see anything quite so elegant, beautiful, and optimistic again? I'm sad to say perhaps not, but that may be the challenge for our great designers, engineers, innovators, and even artists. Can you work together to create something so beautiful, powerful, and iconic it pushes the boundaries of our imagination? Can you make us dream like that again? Can you show us the future?

INTRODUCTION

Conceived in 1962
when technology and
progress were the answers to
everything and the sky was
no longer a limit…

It began with a Concorde model kit. Even disassembled, the swept-back delta wings affixed to the kit frame excited my imagination and motivated me to glue all the pieces together as quickly as possible. The final 1:72 scale version of the world's first commercial supersonic jet awed me and stirred nascent thoughts of becoming a designer someday. Posed dynamically on the kit's accompanying stand, it was the embodiment of pure speed. And not just any speed, but Mach 2—*twice the speed of sound.* Everything about the shape of Concorde announced *FAST.* It made a lasting impression that deepened over the years into a lifelong obsession—if not devotion.

At present my ever-growing collection of Concorde memorabilia encompasses about seven hundred items, including parting gifts informally called "prezzies" that were handed out to the well-fed and well-lubricated passengers who could splurge on the ticket price, which was $12,000 round-trip in 2003. This was swag before swag was a thing. Model kits, stamps, matchbooks, flasks, luggage tags, lighters, and more were given to passengers, while some items were proudly stolen by those besotted with the Concorde lifestyle, such as menus designed by Christian Lacroix (b. 1951) and Jean Boggio (b. 1963), dinnerware by Raymond Loewy (1893–1986), and napkin rings by Sir Terence Conran (b. 1931)—all from the twenty-seven years in which Concorde graced the skies.

Until its last flight in 2003, the silhouette of Concorde streaking through the clouds inspired a rare sense

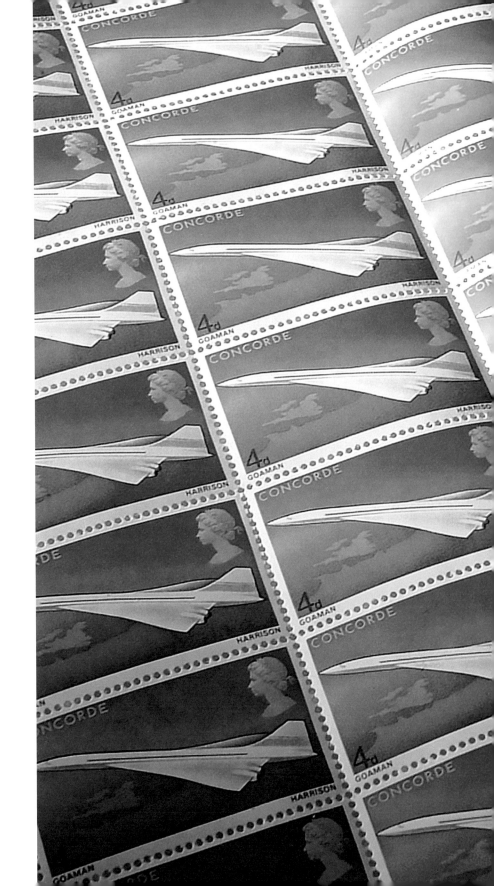

of wonder. Children cheered when they spotted it in the sky. Devotees who lacked the fortune to actually zip through the stratosphere inside its slender fuselage penned poems to honor its soaring beauty. To this day no other form of travel affords passengers the unique experience of flying twice the speed of sound. Passengers on westbound transatlantic flights arrived at their destination at an earlier local time than the time they left their departure city. Regular commercial planes plodding along at 550 mph (885 kmh) a mere 30,000 feet (9000 meters) above ground appeared to travel backward when spied from inside the speeding Concorde. In 1985 a Concorde flight allowed Phil Collins to perform his hits "Against All Odds (Take a Look at Me Now)" and "In the Air Tonight" on the same day at both London's Wembley Stadium and Philadelphia's John F. Kennedy Stadium for the globally televised Live Aid concerts. As German photographer Wolfgang Tillmans rhapsodized in the artist book *Concorde* for his 1997 exhibition *I Didn't Inhale* at London's Chisenhale Gallery:

> Its futuristic shape, speed and ear-numbing thunder grabs people's imagination today as much as it did when it first took off in 1969. It's an environmental nightmare conceived in 1962 when technology and progress was the answer to everything and the sky was no longer a limit... For the chosen few, flying Concorde is apparently a glamorous but cramped and slightly boring routine whilst to watch it in the air, landing or taking-off is a strange and free spectacle, a super modern anachronism and an image of the desire to overcome time and distance through technology.[1]

Despite Concorde's unparalleled success, the flag-waving pride it instilled among the British and French, and the glitzy celebrity of its associated jet-set lifestyle, the at one time fourteen-strong fleet could not fly forever. Only twenty Concordes were ever built, and the six that were not included in the operational fleets of British Airways and Air France were mined for parts. On July 25, 2000, Concorde suffered its only fatal crash during its twenty-seven years in operation. All 109 passengers and crew on board Air France Flight 4590 were killed, as were four people in the hotel it leveled. The accident dealt a devastating blow to an aging fleet. In 2003 British Airways and Air France announced Concorde's official retirement. The crash, along with reduced air travel following the attacks of September 11, 2001, and rising maintenance costs, created an insensible budgetary model. Concorde's last flight departed from John F. Kennedy International Airport in New York for Heathrow Airport in London on October 24, 2003 (Air France's final Concorde flight took place on June 27th). All one hundred seats were sold, and passengers included model Christie Brinkley, actress Joan Collins ("a tragedy, honestly a tragedy!"[2]), and an Ohio couple who had snagged tickets on eBay for $60,000 (one way!). The final flight inspired a local London musical production based on people's Concorde experiences, was greeted by a large crowd of enthusiastic spectators, and elicited a surprising outpouring of grief.

It was as if a glorious future had been glimpsed only to be rejected out of hand. Imagine abandoning lifesaving MRI technology after a few years, or returning our smartphones for the mindfulness of rotary dialing. Yet all is not lost. For some time now NASA has been developing a "low-boom" Quiet Supersonic Transport (QueSST), and flight tests for the "new Concorde" are planned for as early as 2021. In 2015 Airbus filed a patent for a superjet dubbed the "Son of Concorde" that would fly at Mach 4 (2,500 mph/4,023 kmh) and cut the travel time from New York to London to an hour! And a private supersonic jet called the Aerion AS2 is expected to enter service in 2023. Meanwhile, a new breed of visionaries have been spending their billions developing the commercial possibilities of post-supersonic flight. Richard Branson (Virgin Galactic), Elon Musk (SpaceX), and Jeff Bezos (Blue Origin) are promising seemingly fantastic results within a decade or two, such as rocket flights to anywhere on the planet in less than an hour. Notably, their respective promotional campaigns recall the original brochures and advertisements for Concorde in trade magazines, firing up the imagination and playing off the desire to fly ahead of the curve.

2019 marks fifty years since Concorde's first successful test flight on March 2 in 1969. It also marks sixteen years since I experienced my one and only Concorde flight from JFK to Heathrow. What had been earmarked for the "someday" column became an imperative when, just shy of my thirtieth birthday, Concorde announced service would be ending. A native Californian, the 9 a.m. departure out of JFK felt like 6 a.m. to me, and then—in a flash— it was over. In between, I made memories I will never forget: the rapid tranquility of check-in, the quiet elegance of the Concorde room, and the object of fascination, parked and waiting on the tarmac.

I had a window seat. I remember being surprised at how tiny the windows were. But at takeoff was when the difference could really be felt. Every time Concorde departed from JFK, it had to perform a noise abatement maneuver—a sharp roll, turn, then spring out of the turn, almost instantly. I felt like I was in a fighter jet—with a hundred other people. Breaking the sound barrier was barely noticeable. I heard it because I was watching and listening for it—the sound was like someone popped a balloon in the next room. There was lunch, champagne, and flowers in the lavatory. I got the sense that the crew members took great care, and were the best in the field. Even though the fastest flight I had been on was over too quickly, the end of the flight was the real beginning of the journey that led to this book.

As a designer, I'm particularly interested in Concorde's design legacy, from the marvel of its aerodynamic perfection and the refinements of its interior cabin experience to the various and sundry objects designed to support and promote its brand. Some of the most interesting items in my collection are the brochures from the 1970s that contextualize the supersonic jet culture, lifestyle, and fashion. The photography, the graphic language, and the typography are all calibrated to excite an aura of speed, glamour, and progress. Concorde was the promise of tomorrow delivered in the here and now. It's time we fully appreciate the lasting significance of our first—and so far sole— supersonic commercial airliner.

Lawrence Azerrad

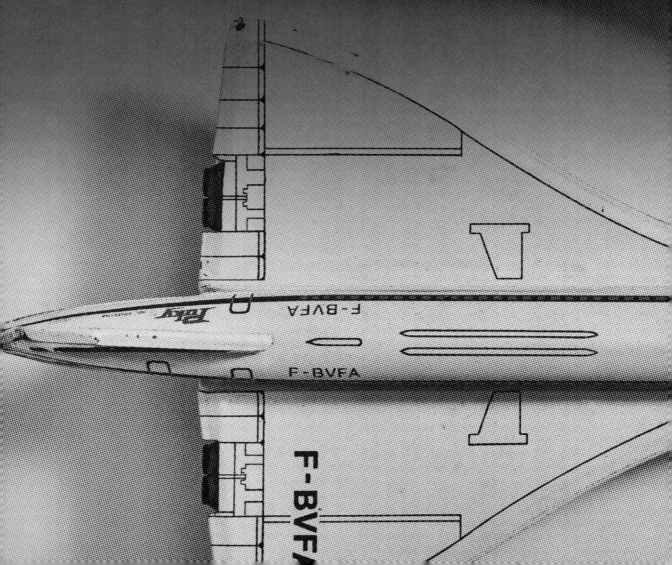

1 | THE DAWN OF THE SUPERSONIC AIRLINER

GPO 1st day cover
CONCORDE

Concorde was the promise
of tomorrow delivered in
the here and now.

Since the advent of powered flight on the North Carolina beaches of Kitty Hawk in 1903—an almost slapstick production when you watch the old reels on YouTube[3]—it could be argued that no passenger plane has captured the public imagination as magnificently as the supersonic Concorde. Affectionately christened *L'Oiseau blanc* (the white bird) by the French, Concorde (smartly dressed without a definite article by the British) graced our skies— at least within the narrow purview of its approved flight paths—for twenty-seven improbable years. From every perspective, our history's sole dalliance with a supersonic passenger plane epitomized the most important equation of our moneyed age: not $E = mc^2$, but time = money. That it did so with such panache only added to its conspicuous luster.

Concorde's signature form aroused the sort of fandom unimaginable for a typical (i.e., economical) subsonic commercial airliner. Concorde was more spacecraft than passenger airplane. Sleek, graceful, and doubly white to deflect the heat of its extraordinary speed, it was an aspirational vision that might have been left on the cutting-room floor of Stanley Kubrick's *2001: A Space Odyssey* (1968). But it was miraculously, gloriously real. As its needle-pointed, delta-winged shape soared toward the stratosphere, one felt touched by the future and its attendant sense of hope and promise, whether on the ground or snug in its luxuriously appointed fuselage. It's what the Space Shuttle *should* have looked like.

OPPOSITE
Detail of Royal Mail First Day
postage cover commemorating
the maiden test flight of
Concorde 001 (see page 74), 1969

RIGHT
Preproduction model Concorde
002 visits Los Angeles
International Airport on a
promotional tour, October 23, 1974

Even the high-powered executives, heads of state, and rock stars who'd seen it all couldn't help but be enthralled by the fighter-jet–like ascent toward 55,000 feet (16,764 meters) (twice the altitude of commercial airplanes) and the truly rare experience of cruising at Mach 2 (1,350 mph/2,172 kmh), roughly twice the average speed of a commercial flight, while viewing the actual curvature of the Earth outside their windows. Not to mention the mind-bending phenomena resulting from the precipitous speeds, such as the cabin stretching by as much as 7 to 10 inches (18 to 25 centimeters) during flight due to the heating of the airframe, or that it traveled 10 miles (16 kilometers) in the time it took to fill a champagne glass.

More than anything, the aura of postwar optimism propelled the development of the world's first supersonic passenger plane. To the public at the time, flying faster than the speed of sound in order to travel from London to New York in just three hours seemed like outright science fiction. But to those inspired by the scientific, mathematical, and technological advances necessitated by World War II, to aim for the impossible was precisely the point. As John F. Kennedy put it in his famous address at Houston's Rice University on September 12, 1962: "We choose to go to the moon in this decade and do the other things, not because they are easy, but because they are hard, because that goal will serve to organize and measure the best of our energies and skills, because that challenge is one that we are willing to accept,

An aura of postwar optimism propelled the development of the world's first supersonic passenger plane.

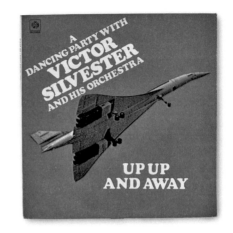

one we are unwilling to postpone, and one which we intend to win." Only seven years later, in 1969, Neil Armstrong added a boot-shaped crater to the surface of the moon. That same year saw the maiden flight of the Boeing 747, whose fuel-efficient seating capacity of 660 helped to popularize the idea of commercial aviation. Seven years after that, on January 21, 1976, the first Concordes with commercial passengers departed simultaneously from Heathrow Airport in London and Orly Airport in Paris.

Though the Space Race had its origins in the nuclear arms race that mired the world in the decades-long Cold War, it laid the groundwork for rapid innovation on a global scale. In fact, from 1950 to 1980 "innovation" became an American buzzword that "was understood as a process: theoretical research in labs provided an initial foundation; applications of that research were devised and developed; and from there, they became commercialized products."[4] Around the world, related buzzwords (in their respective languages) like "progress," "dream," and "tomorrow" flourished, especially in what would later be dubbed the golden age of advertising.

ABOVE
Architectural model of Los Angeles International Airport from Welton Becket & Associates, c. 1960

OPPOSITE
Drawing of Los Angeles International Airport from Welton Becket & Associates (the renderings of the delta-winged aircraft at the gates indicate the expected advent of regular worldwide Concorde travel), c. 1960

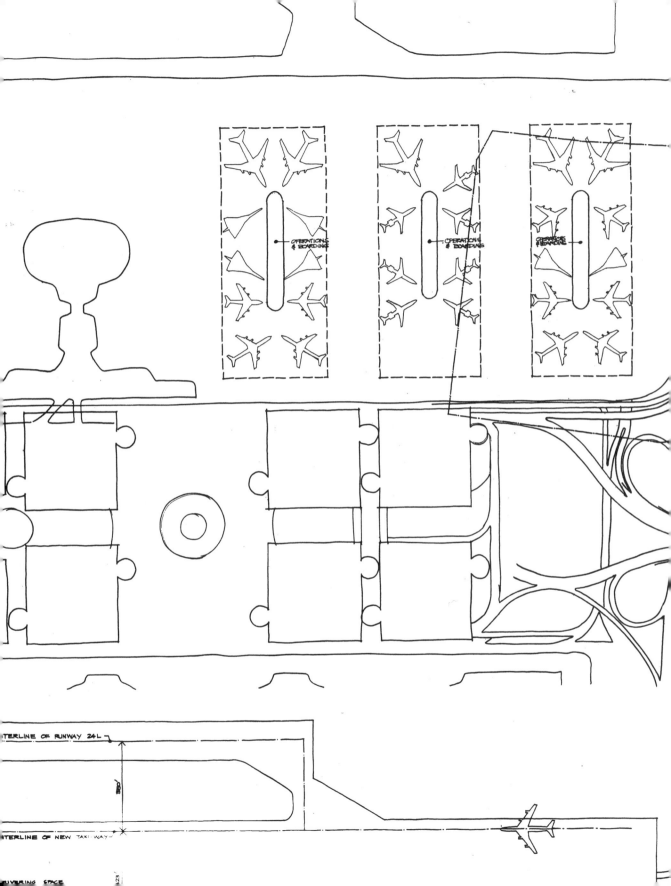

OPERATIONS & BOARDING

OPERATIONS & BOARDING

OPERATIONS & BOARDING

CENTERLINE OF RUNWAY 24L

CENTERLINE OF NEW TAXI WAY

MANEUVERING SPACE

Comparing the SST Designs

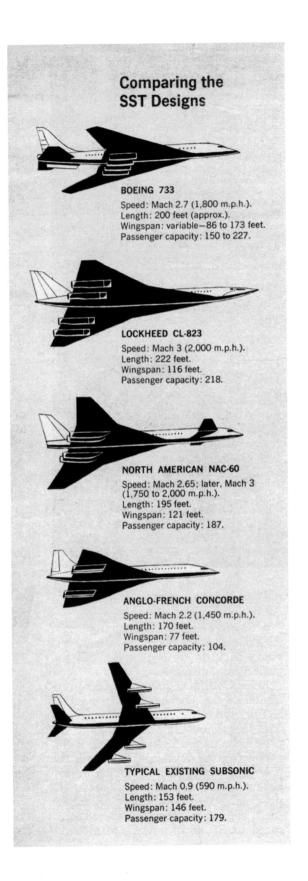

BOEING 733

Speed: Mach 2.7 (1,800 m.p.h.).
Length: 200 feet (approx.).
Wingspan: variable—86 to 173 feet.
Passenger capacity: 150 to 227.

LOCKHEED CL-823

Speed: Mach 3 (2,000 m.p.h.).
Length: 222 feet.
Wingspan: 116 feet.
Passenger capacity: 218.

NORTH AMERICAN NAC-60

Speed: Mach 2.65; later, Mach 3
(1,750 to 2,000 m.p.h.).
Length: 195 feet.
Wingspan: 121 feet.
Passenger capacity: 187.

ANGLO-FRENCH CONCORDE

Speed: Mach 2.2 (1,450 m.p.h.).
Length: 170 feet.
Wingspan: 77 feet.
Passenger capacity: 104.

TYPICAL EXISTING SUBSONIC

Speed: Mach 0.9 (590 m.p.h.).
Length: 153 feet.
Wingspan: 146 feet.
Passenger capacity: 179.

Concorde was more spacecraft than passenger transport.

There was at that time a palpable hopefulness for a better future, a spirit of curiosity and optimism that, if not genuine, was at least reflected in the designs of the age that eventually helped set the stage for supersonic commercial travel. The curved and flowing lines of Eero Saarinen's iconic TWA Terminal (1962) at John F. Kennedy International Airport, for example, explicitly followed the client's design brief to capture the "spirit of flight." As Saarinen (1910–1961) stated during its construction, "all the curves, all the spaces and elements right down to the shape of the signs, display boards, railings and check-in desks were to be of a matching nature. We wanted passengers passing through the building to experience a fully-designed environment."[5] The same could be said verbatim of Concorde's overall design concept in its several iterations. In the same year, Saarinen's swooping, winglike structure of the main terminal for Washington Dulles International Airport was completed. On the opposite coast, the UFO-like Theme Building (1961) at Los Angeles International Airport designed by Pereira & Luckman mirrored the city's dream to become the city of tomorrow, while Walt Disney unveiled the vision for his Experimental Prototype Community of Tomorrow (EPCOT) at the 1964–65 New York World's Fair.

There was a palpable hopefulness for a better future, a spirit of curiosity and optimism.

Disney's four pavilions at the World's Fair advertised the possibility of a fabulous reality in the very near future (if we could all just share in his unflagging zeal). It was a campaign similar to the trade and manufacturer advertisements exhibited in these pages, what were in effect Concorde's early branding efforts to raise awareness of and enthusiasm for the development of the world's first luxury supersonic airliner. (Twenty-first-century visionaries such as Jeff Bezos, Richard Branson, and Elon Musk take the same approach in their respective post-supersonic projects through the use of promotional videos and social media.) The graphic language in these ads capitalizes on postwar sensibilities, cheering us on to "share in its success" and speed forward into a better socioeconomic future. The acute angles and absence of serifed typography, and of course the iconic silhouette of Concorde, suggest design imbued with the idea of progress.

Whether we call the postwar era that laid the groundwork for supersonic aviation the Space Age, the Atomic Age, or define it by the movements of modernism or mid-century modernism, the overall design aesthetic explicitly promised a better world to come. Concorde's emergence as an indisputable

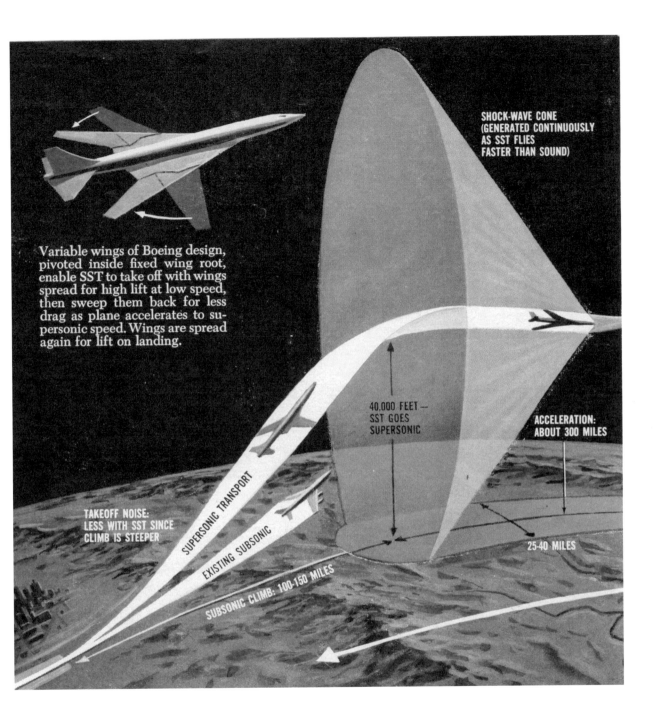

SHOCK-WAVE CONE
(GENERATED CONTINUOUSLY
AS SST FLIES
FASTER THAN SOUND)

Variable wings of Boeing design, pivoted inside fixed wing root, enable SST to take off with wings spread for high lift at low speed, then sweep them back for less drag as plane accelerates to supersonic speed. Wings are spread again for lift on landing.

40,000 FEET —
SST GOES
SUPERSONIC

ACCELERATION:
ABOUT 300 MILES

TAKEOFF NOISE:
LESS WITH SST SINCE
CLIMB IS STEEPER

SUPERSONIC TRANSPORT

EXISTING SUBSONIC

SUBSONIC CLIMB: 100-150 MILES

25-40 MILES

OPPOSITE
Mobil Worldwide Aviation
Service advertisement, c. 1960s

ABOVE
Magazine illustration showing
the altitude and sonic boom
trail for supersonic flight, 1964

Nosing ahead and showing the way

The prototype Concorde aircraft are equipped with a combined Inertial Navigation and Computing System developed by FERRANTI and SAGEM. Pilot control of these systems is simplified by the FERRANTI Automatic Chart Display.

The supersonic transport is setting new requirements in the field of Navigation, Computing and Navigation Display. The systems fitted to the prototype Concordes embody the most modern Instrumental Electronic and Display techniques ever to fly in any civil transport aircraft.

The S.S.T. will operate in a new environment determined both by the aircraft characteristics and the air traffic control system of the 1970's.

The solution of these operational problems necessitates the use of the most modern technologies if the resulting systems are to make a real contribution to the reduction of the pilot's work load in an aircraft which will have to operate across oceans, uninhabited territories and areas of dense air traffic. FERRANTI have always pioneered the latest Electronic and Computing techniques and have the largest and most com-

prehensive microcircuit facilities in Europe. Added to their pioneering work in navigation display this enables them to set the pace in the development and production of a new generation of systems to solve tomorrow's operational problems in the transport aircraft of the future.

Ferranti Ltd., Ferry Road,
Edinburgh 5, Scotland.

First into the Future

icon of modern design may seem like a natural evolution in line with Saarinen's terminals, Charles and Ray Eames's lounge chair and ottoman for Herman Miller, and Oscar Niemeyer's dazzling constructions in Brazil, but the marvel of its technological design and branding excellence belies the many obstacles it had to overcome in order to spread its delta wings—obstacles that finally grounded the entire Concorde enterprise in 2003, one hundred years after the miracle at Kitty Hawk.

OPPOSITE
Computing and navigation
systems manufacturer
Ferranti Concorde engagement
advertisement, 1968

ABOVE
Concorde prototype in British
Overseas Airways Corporation
(BOAC) livery, c. 1960s

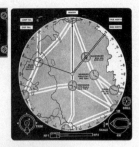

FERRANTI
AUTOMATIC CHART DISPLAY
CHOSEN FOR CONCORDE

**THE FERRANTI AUTOMATIC CHART DISPLAY
IS THE ONLY PICTORIAL NAVIGATION DISPLAY
TO PROVIDE ALL THESE FACILITIES:**

☐ operates on inputs from self-contained or ground-based navaids: inertial;
Doppler; long-range radio aids such as Loran C; VOR/DME; etc.
☐ cross monitors between self-contained and external navaids or between two
self-contained aids
☐ world-wide coverage together with extensive storage of data sheets
☐ co-ordinate insertion and flight-plan check
☐ four scales to meet requirements for en-route and terminal-area conditions
☐ north-oriented or track-oriented display

Acting as the vital input/output interface between pilot and computer, the Automatic
Chart Display will form an essential part of modern navigation systems and will make
a significant contribution to the operational flexibility required in the modern ATC
environment.
In the Concorde, the Ferranti Automatic Chart Display will be integrated with the
SAGEM/Ferranti digital-inertial navigation system.

FERRANTI
First into the Future

ENQUIRIES TO : **FERRANTI LTD** • **FERRY ROAD** • **EDINBURGH** • **SCOTLAND** • **Tel: (031) DEAn 1211**

INTERAVIA 6/1966 841

ABOVE
Concorde ashtray, 1968

OPPOSITE, TOP
Magazine article announcing
the never-realized Air Canada
Concorde service, 1967

OPPOSITE, BOTTOM
Aerospace manufacturer
Plessey Company Ltd
advertisement, 1968

Seven Months To The Sonic Boom

The Concorde (full-scale model above, artist's impression at right) will travel at more than twice the speed of sound.

The Concorde, the world's first supersonic airliner, is an engineering marvel—but when it's in high gear it will lay down a carpet of ear-shattering noise perhaps 60 miles wide. And Air Canada has four on order

By Stephen Franklin
Weekend Magazine

LONDON. ONLY SEVEN MONTHS from now on Feb. 28, 1968, the world's first supersonic airliner, the Concorde prototype 001, is scheduled to scream down a runway at Toulouse, France, and roar into the air on its initial test flight. If all goes well, the 1,450-m.p.h. Concorde will go into regular passenger service on the transatlantic run three years later. And life for millions of people may never be the same again.

Travelling 10 miles up in the stratosphere at more than twice the speed of sound — which is 660 m.p.h. at 60,000 feet — the thin droop-nose airliner will make the flight from Montreal to London in about three hours and 10 minutes, shrinking the geography of the world like a woollen sweater put in a clothes dryer. It will

also annihilate time, making it possible to finish a cigar and leisurely after dinner in England and still be home in your Canadian living room in time for Hockey Night in Canada, because of the time difference.

It may also make stay-at-homes on quiet suburban streets imagine they are living next door to an African tom-tom factory and drive the busiest of sleepers to the drug store in search of ear plugs. For every time a Concorde passes overhead at supersonic speed it will unroll behind it a sonic-boom carpet 40 to 60 miles wide and perhaps 3,000 miles long. Contrary to popular belief, the sonic boom does not occur only at the moment the plane breaks through the sound barrier, but happens all the time the aircraft is flying faster than sound, which will be

80 per cent of its time in the air if the airlines have their way.

Nobody knows for sure how loud the sonic boom from the Concorde and other SSTs (supersonic transports) like the Russian TU-144 and the Boeing 2707 will be. It depends on the airliner's size and weight and on how high it is flying, but the boom carpet will certainly be the noisiest broadfront in existence. As Edwin Brooks, a British M.P., said to the House of Commons: "The SST is still in the age of the silent film. It has yet to have the sound track added."

The sonic boom may be only as loud and startling as a car door slammed hard and unexpectedly three feet from your left eardrum or it may be a Jovian thunderbolt calculated to make coffee cups dance

Photo illustration by Julius Seelar and Gábor Dispensieri — Weekend Magazine

Continued on page 4

this should come as no surprise

BOAC
TAKES GOOD CARE OF YOU

Four Olympus engines will propel Concorde at 1,450mph —800mph faster than any airliner flying today.

BRISTOL SIDDELEY and SNECMA SUPPLY THE POWER Bristol Siddeley Engines Limited, London.

La Société Nationale d'Etude
et de Construction de Moteurs d'Aviation, Paris.

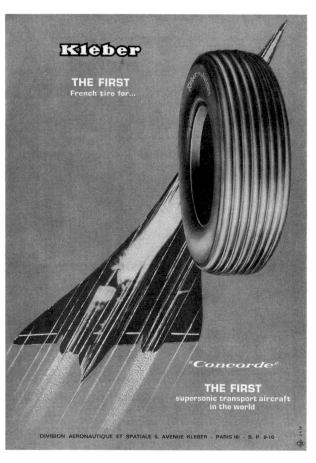

Kléber

THE FIRST
French tire for...

"Concorde"

THE FIRST
supersonic transport aircraft
in the world

DIVISION AERONAUTIQUE ET SPATIALE 6, AVENUE KLEBER - PARIS 16ᵉ · B. P. 9-16

Kléber-Colombes
AEROSPACE DIVISION

WILL BE YOUR BEST CHOICE
ON
Concorde

6, AVENUE KLEBER - PARIS 19ᵉ
TELEPHONE : 555.01.00
TELEX Nᵒ 28.811

Kléber-Colombes est prêt !

Après Caravelle, Boeing 707, D.C. 8, etc...
Kléber-Colombes
offre pour Concorde
le premier pneu étudié,
développé et fabriqué en France.

DIVISION AERONAUTIQUE ET SPATIALE

Kléber-Colombes

6, AVENUE KLEBER - PARIS 16ᵉ - KLE 00.01 - B.P. 9.16

THIS PAGE
Kléber Concorde tire
advertisements, 1966–69

OPPOSITE
Dunlop Concorde tire
advertisement, 1968

Between ourselves, we're pretty bucked that Dunlop tyres were chosen for both the British and French versions of the Concorde. To say nothing of the wheels they're fitted to, the brakes that control them, and quite a number of other vital operational and constructional components, such as jet engine controls, windscreen wiper system and parachute brake release unit. It's good to know there's international agreement about the quality and reliability of Dunlop aviation equipment.

Why Dunlop? Because this world-embracing organisation has the greatest experience; it has equipped the Comet, the VC.10, the Jetstream ... over 100 different types of aircraft operated by over 400 world airlines, corporate operators, and air forces ... and because it operates a world-wide product support and service network. These are the things that engender confidence and win contracts—internationally.

CONCORDE FLIES *DUNLOP*

 THE DUNLOP COMPANY LIMITED · AVIATION DIVISION · FOLESHILL · COVENTRY

Dunlop have long been in the forefront of British companies who are eager to co-operate with European aircraft manufacturers. Among the latest international projects with which the Company are associated is the Anglo-French 'Concorde'. Major items of Dunlop equipment supplied for this supersonic civil aircraft include tyres, wheels, brakes, brake control systems, engine controls, and windscreen wiper systems.

THE DUNLOP COMPANY LIMITED · AVIATION DIVISION · HOLBROOK LANE · FOLESHILL · COVENTRY

Mach 2

Mach 2 *has become routine*

Concorde 001

"...the strongest challenger to American domination of the international transport market in history".
Aviation Week editorial, February 8th, 1971

designed and built by **AEROSPATIALE FRANCE** and **BRITISH AIRCRAFT CORPORATION**

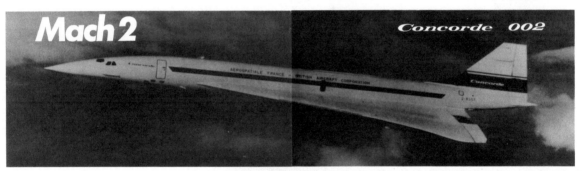

Mach 2

Concorde 002

Circle Number 47 on Reader-Service Card

RADIO ALTIMETERS

TRT

OPPOSITE
Dunlop Concorde tire
advertisement, 1968

ABOVE
Aérospatiale France and British
Aircraft Corporation Concorde
001 and 002 prototype
advertisement, 1971

RIGHT
Télécommunications Radioélec-
triques et Téléphoniques radio
altimeters advertisement, 1966

Forward landing gear,
steering control and tail bumper
for the **CONCORDE SST**, produced by **MESSIER**.

MESSIER

58, RUE FÉNELON - 92 - MONTROUGE   Téléphone : 253 22-36

INTERAVIA 5/1968 833

DOWTY

on the Concorde

Powered Flying Controls
and Servo-Hydraulic Equipment

DOWTY GROUP LIMITED · CHELTENHAM · GLOS · ENGLAND

120 INTERAVIA 2/1968

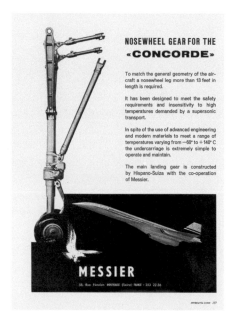

NOSEWHEEL GEAR FOR THE
«CONCORDE»

To match the general geometry of the aircraft a nosewheel leg more than 13 feet in
length is required.

It has been designed to meet the safety
requirements and insensitivity to high
temperatures demanded by a supersonic
transport.

In spite of the use of advanced engineering
and modern materials to meet a range of
temperatures varying from —60° to +140° C
the undercarriage is extremely simple to
operate and maintain.

The main landing gear is constructed
by Hispano-Suiza with the co-operation
of Messier.

MESSIER

58, Rue Fénelon MONTROUGE (Seine) FRANCE · 253 22-36

INTERAVIA 5/1968 137

ABOVE
Dowty Concorde hydraulic
equipment advertisement,
1968

**ABOVE, LEFT and
LEFT**
Messier Concorde landing
gear advertisements, 1969

OPPOSITE
British Aircraft Corporation
and Sud Aviation France
Concorde advertisement
announcing participating
airlines, 1968

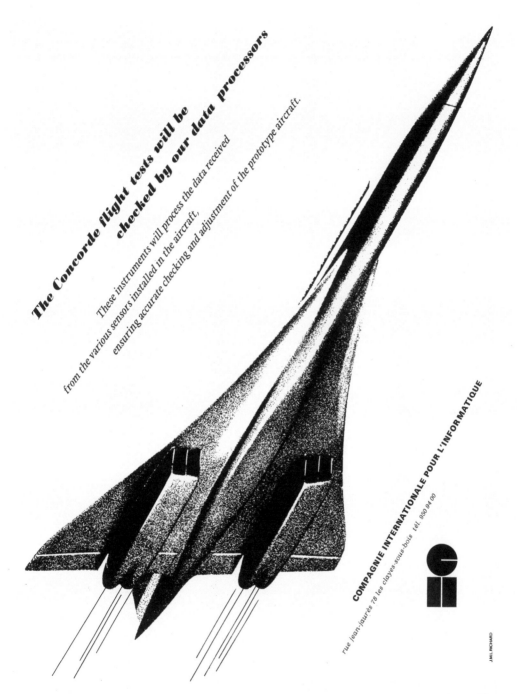

The Concorde flight tests will be checked by our data processors

These instruments will process the data received from the various sensors installed in the aircraft, ensuring accurate checking and adjustment of the prototype aircraft.

COMPAGNIE INTERNATIONALE POUR L'INFORMATIQUE

rue jean-jaurès 78 les clayes-sous-bois tél. 950 94 00

J.M.L. RICHARD

On flights to more than 60 of the world's cities,
Concorde has proved its ability to halve journey-times

worldbeaters

CONCORDE –supersonic intercontinental airliner
built by BAC and Aérospatiale

JAGUAR –low-level tactical strike and reconnaissance aircraft
built by BAC and Dassault/Breguet

MRCA –multi-role combat aircraft
built by BAC, Messerschmitt-Bölkow-Blohm and Aeritalia

RAPIER –ultra-low-level missile air defence system
built by British Aircraft Corporation

...each at the top of its class

BRITISH AIRCRAFT CORPORATION
the spearhead of technological achievement

BAC 363 2/75

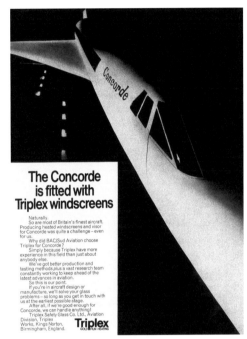

The Concorde is fitted with Triplex windscreens

Naturally.
So are most of Britain's finest aircraft.
Producing heated windscreens and visor for Concorde was quite a challenge – even for us.
Why did BAC/Sud Aviation choose Triplex for Concorde?
Simply because Triplex have more experience in this field than just about anybody else.
We've got better production and testing methods plus a vast research team constantly working to keep ahead of the latest advances in aviation.
So this is our point.
If you're in aircraft design or manufacture, we'll solve your glass problems – so long as you get in touch with us at the earliest possible stage.
After all, if we're good enough for Concorde, we can handle anything!
Triplex Safety Glass Co. Ltd., Aviation Division, Triplex Works, Kings Norton, Birmingham, England.

Triplex GOLD FILM HEATING

FROM THE E28/39 TO THE CONCORDE

NIMONIC *
alloys by Wiggin

The first NIMONIC alloy was developed in 1940 for the Whittle gas turbine engine, used in the Gloster-Whittle E28/39. Today, various NIMONIC alloys from a range of sixteen are chosen for such famous engines as: the Rolls-Royce Bristol SNECMA Olympus 593 for Concorde; Rolls-Royce RB211 for the TriStar; Rolls-Royce Turbomeca Adour for Jaguar; Rolls-Royce Bristol SNECMA M45H for the German/Dutch VFW 614.

The range of NIMONIC alloys has been developed especially for high-stress components operating at high temperatures, and where creep-resistance is particularly important.

They are available in all the usual wrought forms, and also partly processed towards the finished component stage.

Only Henry Wiggin have thirty years experience in this highly specialised field.

* NIMONIC is a HENRY WIGGIN trademark
For full technical details of the NIMONIC alloy range please contact:

HENRY WIGGIN & COMPANY LTD
NIMONIC ALLOYS
HEREFORD, ENGLAND.
Telephone: Hereford 6461 Telex: 35101

OPPOSITE
Sud Aviation SST prototype
Super-Caravelle
advertisement, 1964

ABOVE
British Aircraft Corporation
advertisement, 1975

ABOVE, RIGHT
Triplex Safety Glass Concorde
windscreen advertisement, 1969

RIGHT
Nimonic alloy manufacturer
Henry Wiggin & Company
advertisement, 1969

The iconic silhouette was
imbued with the idea of progress.

Olympus 593
just before the dawn

Concorde is now flying regularly out of Toulouse
and Fairford. Propelled smoothly through the most
exacting test programme any aircraft has ever undergone,
by four Olympus 593 engines.
The Olympus 593 is already helping to make history.
Soon it will be part of everyday life for the airlines of the world.
The dawn is very near.

Rolls-Royce Limited, Bristol Engine Division,
P.O. Box 3, Filton, Bristol, England.
Société Nationale d'Etude et de Construction de Moteurs d'Aviation,
150 Boulevard Haussman, Paris VIIIe., France.

Photograph by courtesy of B.A.C. Filton.

If you were flying the Concorde tomorrow

you'd wear a Rolex.

When the Concorde takes off on its experimental flights through the sound barrier, the watch on board will be Rolex.

Its tough Oyster® case is carved out of a block of 18kt. Gold or Swedish stainless steel. Inside these solid walls is a self-winding, officially certified 30-jewel Swiss chronometer. And outside, its face tells the date and the time in two time zones at once.

It took three years to build the first Concorde. And it takes over a year to build every Rolex Oyster Perpetual. Care like this spells precision—Pan Am® pilots who will fly the Concorde could not afford to settle for less.

The Rolex these pilots wear is the GMT-Master Chronometer. In 18kt. gold with matching bracelet, $1,125. In steel, $255.

*Individually tested and guaranteed to a depth of 165 feet when case, crown and crystal are intact.
Official Timepiece, Pan American World Airways.
Pan American will be the first U.S. airline to fly the Concorde in scheduled service.

ROLEX

TOP
Concorde pin, c. 1970s

BOTTOM
Metropolitan Police Concorde
cloisonné lapel pin, 2003

OPPOSITE
Die-cast Concorde toys in British
Overseas Airways Corporation
(BOAC), Pan Am, and Air France
liveries, c. 1960s

The overall design aesthetic explicitly
promised a better world to come.

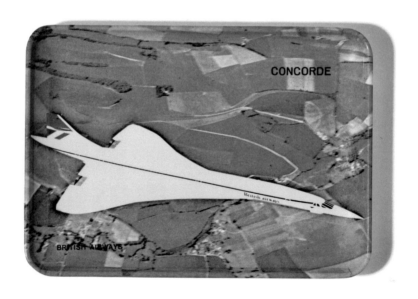

THIS PAGE
Concorde gift trays, c. 1970s

OPPOSITE
Sewing thimble with orbiting
Concorde mechanism, c. 1970s

2

DESIGN: THE LOOK AND FEEL OF CONCORDE

1956–60

The miracle of
Concorde is that
its revolutionary,
iconic design is
purely functional.

When American architect Louis Sullivan set out his principles of design in an 1896 essay, his phrase "form ever follows function" became the overarching motto of modernist design in the twentieth century. And if one were to look for an object that truly defined that rubric, between 1976 and 2003 all one had to do was gaze up at the sky in London, Paris, New York, Washington, DC, and Barbados to glimpse a Concorde roaring, then booming, into the blue—and marvel at how perfectly the jetliner's form encapsulated the speed of sound.

But Concorde is not only a near-perfect feat of form following function, it is also an emblem of survival— and of possibility. To get off the ground, it would have to overcome multiple technological, environmental,

political, and economic challenges—impediments that ultimately clipped American and Soviet attempts at supersonic commercial flight[6]—and rely on the cooperative talents and hard work of countless engineers, designers, scientists, and politicians, as well as a healthy dose of luck.

On the engineering side, advances in fighter-jet technology during World War II rapidly pushed the speed envelope. Though British aviation particularly excelled in this area, it was American pilot Chuck Yeager who first broke the sound barrier, flying the experimental Bell X-1 at Mach 1 (767 mph/1,234 kmh) on October 14, 1947. Six years later another American pilot, Albert Scott Crossfield, cracked the Mach 2 barrier. Achieving supersonic speed

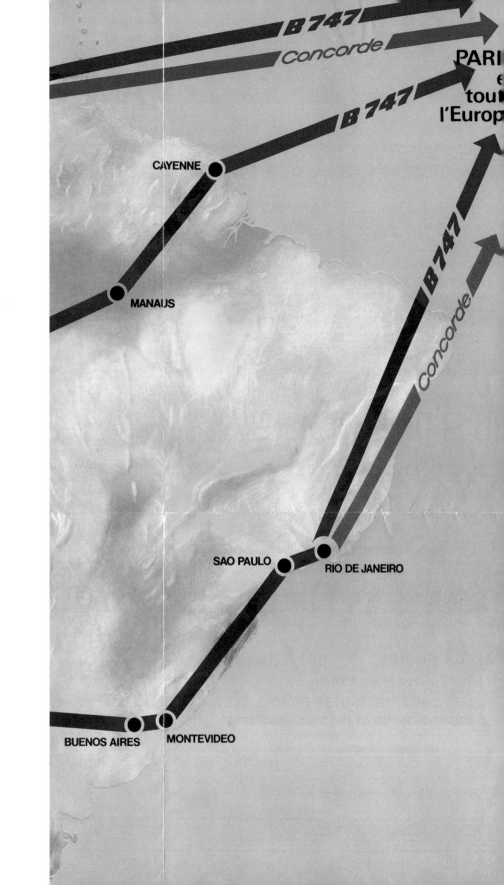

ANGLO - FRENCH SUPERSONIC TRANSPORT PROJECT, "CONCORD"

MODEL MADE IN WORKSHOPS AT
R. A. E. BEDFORD

HANDLEY

Mr. Hanson, director of the
Royal Aircraft Establishment in
Bedford, England, with a scale
model of Concorde, 1964

wasn't the obstacle; the challenge was applying it to a commercial passenger enterprise that was also economically and environmentally viable.

On November 5, 1956, Sir Morien Morgan of the Royal Aircraft Establishment (RAE) convened the first meeting of the Supersonic Transport Aircraft Committee (STAC) in Farnborough, Hampshire, England. While British aviation had excelled during the Second World War, America had taken the lead in commercial passenger aviation after the war with the success of the Boeing 707 and the Douglas DC-8 airliners. Britain, long accustomed to its status as a world power, found itself with much ground to recover in the commercial aviation industry, especially after the well-publicized failures of its de Havilland DH 106 Comet, the world's first commercial jetliner. As Morgan put it, the development of a supersonic aircraft would enable the British "to look the Americans firmly in the eye again."[7]

While British engineers carried out feasibility studies on a series of supersonic transports (SSTs) that culminated in the Bristol Type 223, Sud Aviation in France had also developed an SST called the Super-Caravelle that was essentially a much smaller version of Concorde. But by 1960 funding had reached an impasse for both the French and the British SST programs as political opposition—specifically to the extraordinary cost and the environmental noise pollution—threatened to shut down research. A solution arrived when the British and French governments signed an international treaty to jointly develop an SST. Subsequent to signing the treaty, a consortium between the British Aircraft Corporation and Aérospatiale France was established and prototype testing began in earnest, especially after orders were secured for more than a hundred new airliners from most of the world's major airlines.

The miracle of Concorde is that its revolutionary, iconic design is purely functional. The physics of the craft informs its shape. The needle-shaped fuselage, the adjustable droop snoot, the swept-back delta wing planform, the vertical tail design, the small

OPPOSITE
A team of designers examine a
Concorde cabin, April 1964

ABOVE
A model lineup of the various
designs suggested for the
shape of Concorde (the final
design is at the far end), 1964

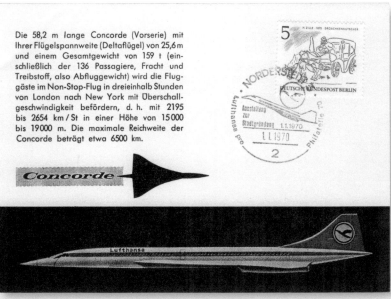

Die 58,2 m lange Concorde (Vorserie) mit
Ihrer Flügelspannweite (Deltaflügel) von 25,6 m
und einem Gesamtgewicht von 159 t (ein-
schließlich der 136 Passagiere, Fracht und
Treibstoff, also Abfluggewicht) wird die Flug-
gäste im Non-Stop-Flug in dreieinhalb Stunden
von London nach New York mit Überschall-
geschwindigkeit befördern, d. h. mit 2195
bis 2654 km / St in einer Höhe von 15 000
bis 19 000 m. Die maximale Reichweite der
Concorde beträgt etwa 6500 km.

windows, the angelic-white livery—all of it coalesced into an object of speed, power, and grace. There was not one decorative element. Yet by some stroke of luck, the final product remains a timeless beauty. (Perhaps the only element that hasn't aged well is the cluttered analog display of its flight deck.) Compare it to other gravity-defying marvels like the Apollo program rockets, the Space Shuttle, or the Airbus A380, each of which succeeded admirably in its respective purpose while leaving much to be desired in terms of design elegance.

Elegance very much defined the atmosphere inside a Concorde flight. As it approached Mach 1 just twelve minutes after takeoff, the wall of air pressure that built up ahead of the craft required the needle-nose design to punch through the increasing resistance in order to reach the craft's cruising speed of Mach 2. The transition would be as smooth as the surface of the champagne already poured. If flying from London to New York, the first officer advised passengers to set their watches back one and a quarter hour—landing in New York over an hour (local time) before their London departure time. Excitable first-time passengers might applaud as the digital readout on the bulkhead displayed "Mach 2." By this time the droop snoot had mechanically straightened out as the pilot no longer needed to see the runway. The delta wing design created the stability to transition from subsonic to supersonic speed, and handled the pressure of its steep rate of climb. The passport-size windows maximized structural integrity and afforded a rare view of deepest indigo. And the mirror-polish of the all-white livery reduced drag and helped deflect the high thermal conditions.

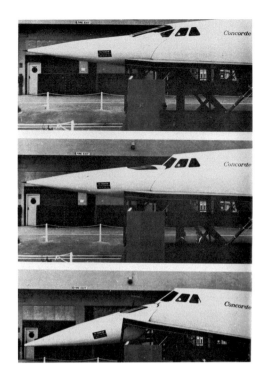

The dimensions of Concorde's two interior cabins were snug. The front sat forty passengers and the rear sixty (the crew included six flight attendants manning seven galleys, two pilots, and one flight engineer). The center aisle was only 16 inches (41 centimeters) wide and provided a few inches clearance above average height. The two seats flanking either side of the aisle were narrower than one might expect and specially designed to withstand the added g-loading caused by Concorde's steep ascent at 1,000 feet (305 meters) per minute, but a series of design upgrades over the jet's lifetime utilized every inch for maximum comfort and luxury. The overhead storage bin was just spacious enough for a high-powered briefcase and possibly a small carry-on, but certainly not a large rolling suit-case. While not as roomy as present-day, subsonic, business-class cabins, the passenger experience was heightened by the short travel time, refinements in comfort, top flight amenities, and the occasional sing-along with Paul McCartney.[8]

ABOVE
Preproduction Concorde in test flight, 1969

RIGHT
Preproduction Concorde demonstrating the visor and nose positions, 1969

True to its name, Concorde was also a miracle of cooperation, its construction dependent on myriad contractors and subcontractors. France designed and built the wing, as well as the flight controls and other associated systems. Since the British had produced the Rolls-Royce Olympus engine that would power Concorde, they were in charge of its design and development, as well as the nose and visor, tail, brakes, and wheels. Yet despite its irrefutable technological success, Concorde almost never got off the ground. Due to the remaining economic, environmental, and political challenges, Concorde's flight paths were severely restricted. Every airline that had initially put in an order backed out. In the end only twenty Concordes were built, of which only fourteen were actually put into service by British Airways and Air France. It was a small fleet compared to most subsonic commercial airliners, but what Concorde lacked in quantity, it would go on to make up for in quality.

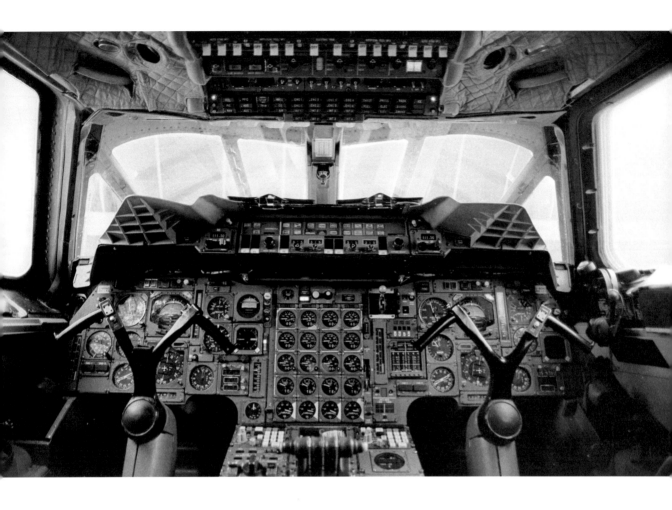

OPPOSITE
First Day postage cover
commemorating the British
Overseas Airways Corporation
(BOAC) Concorde, 1969

ABOVE
British Airways Concorde
cockpit, 2003

67

OPPOSITE, TOP
Pan Am Concorde and US SST
advertisement, 1969

OPPOSITE, BOTTOM
Pan Am matchbook interior
promoting Concorde service,
1969

THIS PAGE
Pan Am matchbooks promoting
the supersonic Jet Clipper and
its destinations, 1969

SPRING 1974

Supersonic Age

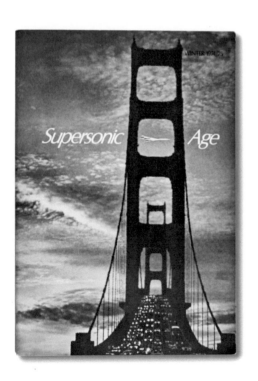

WINTER 1974/75

Supersonic Age

SUMMER 1974

Supersonic Age

Claude Monpoint, Air France Chief Steward, has already flown over 100 hours on Concorde, providing first-class cabin service to the VIPs who have been carried on supersonic demonstration flights. We asked him to give his views on "Service, Concorde style".

The transition to Mach 2 would be as smooth as the surface of the champagne on board.

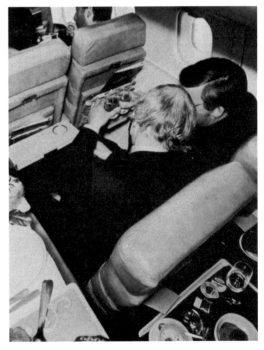

OPPOSITE, THIS PAGE, and FOLLOWING PAGES
Covers and interior images of *Supersonic Age* magazine promoting the development of Concorde service, 1974

71

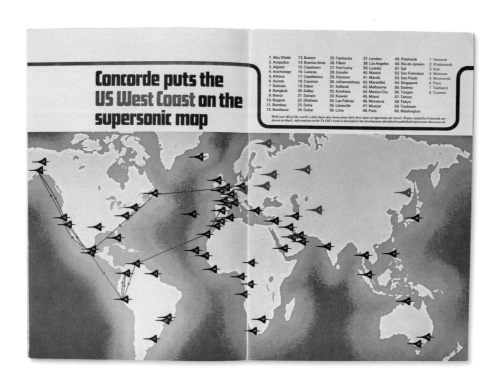

Concorde puts the US West Coast on the supersonic map

1. Abu Dhabi	13. Boston	25. Fairbanks	37. London	49. Prestwick	1. Hanover
2. Acapulco	14. Buenos Aires	26. Filton	38. Los Angeles	50. Rio de Janeiro	2. Khabarovsk
3. Algiers	15. Capetown	27. Fort Lamy	39. Luanda	51. Sal	3. Kiev
4. Anchorage	16. Caracas	28. Gander	40. Madrid	52. San Francisco	4. Moscow
5. Athens	17. Casablanca	29. Hanover	41. Manila	53. Sao Paulo	5. Murmansk
6. Azores	18. Cayenne	30. Johannesburg	42. Marseilles	54. Singapore	6. Paris
7. Bahrain	19. Dakar	31. Keflavik	43. Melbourne	55. Sydney	7. Tashkent
8. Bangkok	20. Dallas	32. Kinshasa	44. Mexico City	56. Tangier	8. Tyumen
9. Beirut	21. Darwin	33. Kuwait	45. Miami	57. Tehran	
10. Bogota	22. Dhahran	34. Las Palmas	46. Monrovia	58. Tokyo	
11. Bombay	23. Doha	35. Libreville	47. Muscat	59. Toulouse	
12. Bordeaux	24. Dubai	36. Lima	48. Paris	60. Washington	

Well over 60 of the world's cities have now been given their first taste of supersonic air travel. Points visited by Concorde are shown in black; information on the Tu 144's visits is incomplete but destinations identified in published reports are shown in red.

Facing page: production of nose and rear fuselages and tail fins for the twin final assembly lines in Britain and France.
1. nose-on view of a Concorde under assembly;
2. part of the British final assembly line;
3. working on the service door to the rear galley;
4. checking a main undercarriage unit.

The Concorde production programme so far authorised by the British and French Governments covers the completion of the first 16 airline-standard aircraft. In addition to these aircraft – eight being assembled at Filton and eight at Toulouse – authorisation has been given for long-dated materials for a further six. The photographs on these and the following pages reveal the impressive production progress already achieved on the airliners which will share the introduction of the first commercial supersonic air services.

Getting *Concorde* into service

19

Concorde is not only a near-perfect feat of form following function, it is an emblem of possibility.

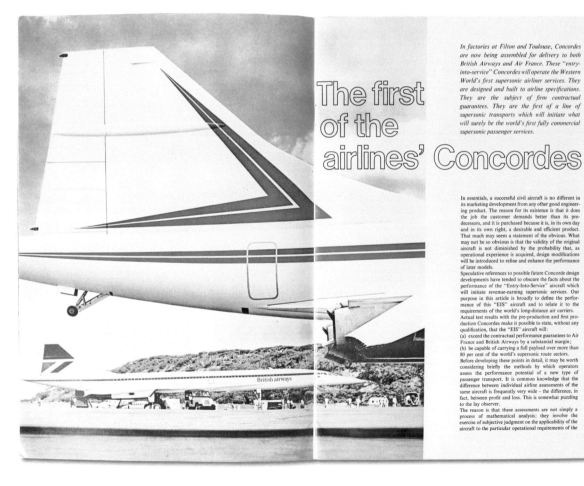

British airways

The first of the airlines' Concordes

In factories at Filton and Toulouse, Concordes are now being assembled for delivery to both British Airways and Air France. These "entry-into-service" Concordes will operate the Western World's first supersonic airliner services. They are designed and built to airline specifications. They are the subject of firm contractual guarantees. They are the first of a line of supersonic transports which will initiate what will surely be the world's first fully commercial supersonic passenger services.

In essentials, a successful civil aircraft is no different in its marketing development from any other good engineering product. The reason for its existence is that it does the job the customer demands better than its predecessors, and it is purchased because it is, in its own day and in its own right, a desirable and efficient product. That much may seem a statement of the obvious. What may not be so obvious is that the validity of the original aircraft is not diminished by the probability that, as operational experience is acquired, design modifications will be introduced to refine and enhance the performance of later models.

Speculative references to possible future Concorde design developments have tended to obscure the facts about the performance of the "Entry-Into-Service" aircraft which will initiate revenue-earning supersonic services. Our purpose in this article is broadly to define the performance of this "EIS" aircraft and to relate it to the requirements of the world's long-distance air carriers. Actual test results with the pre-production and first production Concordes make it possible to state, without any qualification, that the "EIS" aircraft will:

(a) exceed the contractual performance guarantees to Air France and British Airways by a substantial margin;

(b) be capable of carrying a full payload over more than 80 per cent of the world's supersonic route sectors.

Before developing these points in detail, it may be worth considering briefly the methods by which operators assess the performance potential of a new type of passenger transport. It is common knowledge that the difference between individual airline assessments of the same aircraft is frequently very wide – the difference, in fact, between profit and loss. This is somewhat puzzling to the lay observer.

The reason is that these assessments are not simply a process of mathematical analysis; they involve the exercise of subjective judgment on the applicability of the aircraft to the particular operational requirements of the

GPO 1st day cover
CONCORDE

001

9d
GENTLEMAN

Concorde
HARRISON

D. BRADSHAW.

1 RADFORD STREET.

DERBY.

DE 2. 8 NT.

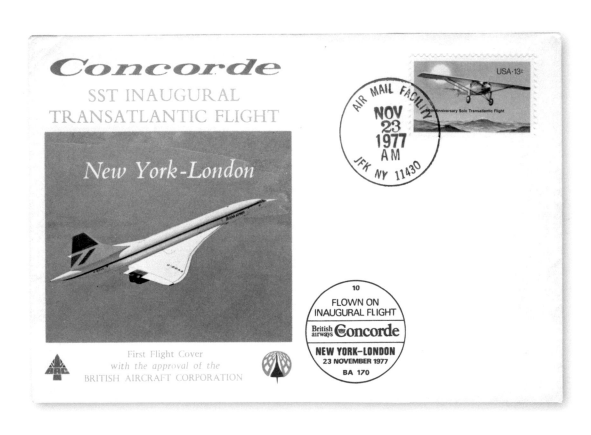

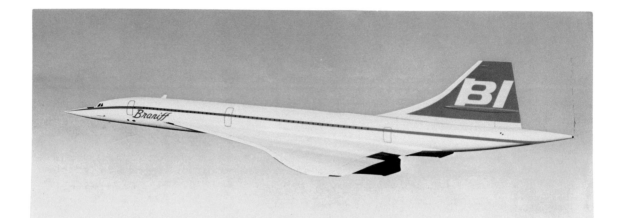

Concorde
<u>between</u> Dallas-Fort Worth <u>and</u>
London—Paris—Washington

- Only Service By Day To Europe
- Washington In Time For Luncheon
- Daily Eastbound Except Monday & Thursday

- Fastest Service From Europe
- First Concorde Flights Within The USA
- Daily Westbound From Washington Except Wednesday and Sunday

Braniff Concorde Service
Concorde flights from Dallas-Fort Worth to London, Paris and Washington began January 13, 1979 with service five days a week to Washington, three days a week to London and twice weekly to Paris. Braniff crews fly the Texas-Washington segment and British Airways and Air France crews the transatlantic segments. This is the only service from Mid-America, the fastest service from Europe to Mid-America, the first Concorde service within the USA. Braniff is the first airline outside Britain and France to fly Concorde.

Total flight time from Dallas-Fort Worth to Paris or London is about seven hours including the stop at Washington. Between DFW and Washington, Concorde flies at the subsonic speed of Mach 0.95 which is 650 miles per hour or 100 miles an hour faster than other jets (almost 20%). From Washington to Paris and London the Concorde flies at supersonic speeds of Mach 2.0 (1,350 miles per hour) for a transatlantic flight time of less than 4 hours. This compares to other jets which fly the Atlantic at less than 600 miles per hour in about 7 hours.

Concorde only has 100 seats. In each of the two cabins there is a digital display or Machmeter showing the speed at which the plane is flying.

Braniff 747 London Service
The Concorde flights complement the only daily 747 non-stop service from Dallas-Fort Worth and the Southwest to Britain and Europe. (Braniff non-stop and through-plane service to Paris, Amsterdam and Brussels from Dallas-Fort Worth will be inaugurated during 1979.) The result is a choice of departure times from Dallas-Fort Worth with Concorde leaving in the morning and the 747 leaving in the early evening. Likewise there is a choice of arrival times and airports in London with Concorde arriving at London Heathrow in the evening and the 747 arriving London Gatwick in morning. There is the same choice on returning flights with the 747 departing London Gatwick late morning and the Concorde departing London Heathrow and Paris Charles DeGaulle in the evening.

Concorde Service Dallas-Fort Worth — Washington — London
(in cooperation with British Airways)
Leave 8:30 AM Dallas-Fort Worth
Arrive 11:45 AM Washington Dulles Terminal
Arrive 9:40 PM London Heathrow
    Wednesday, Friday, Sunday
Concorde Service London — Washington — Dallas-Fort Worth
Leave 6:30 PM London Heathrow
Leave 6:40 PM Washington Dulles Terminal
Arrive 8:30 PM Dallas-Fort Worth
    Tuesday, Thursday, Saturday
Concorde Service Dallas-Fort Worth — Washington — Paris
(in cooperation with Air France)
Leave 9:30 AM Dallas-Fort Worth
Arrive 12:45 PM Washington Dulles Terminal
Arrive 11:35 PM Paris Charles deGaulle
    Tuesday, Saturday
Concorde Service Paris — Washington — Dallas-Fort Worth
Leave 8:00 PM Paris Charles de Gaulle
Leave 7:10 PM Washington Dulles Terminal
Arrive 9:00 PM Dallas-Fort Worth
    Monday, Friday
Braniff 747 Service Dallas-Fort Worth — London
Leave 6:45 PM Arrive 9:15 AM London Gatwick
    Daily Non-stop
Braniff 747 Service London — Dallas-Fort Worth
Leave 11:45 AM London Gatwick Arrive 3:05 PM
    Daily Non-stop
Air Fares.
The premium Concorde service on the international segments is only 20% over normal first class, on the Texas-Washington segment only 10% or $15 more than first class.
For reservations call your travel agent, corporate travel department or Braniff. Air France or British Airways.

Braniff International U.S. Mainland, Hawaii, Alaska, Mexico, South America and Europe

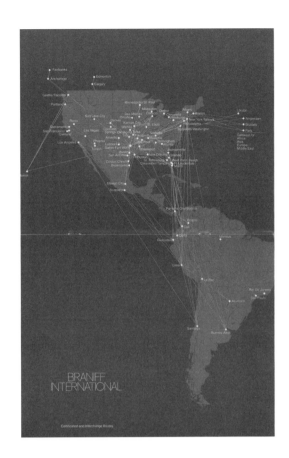

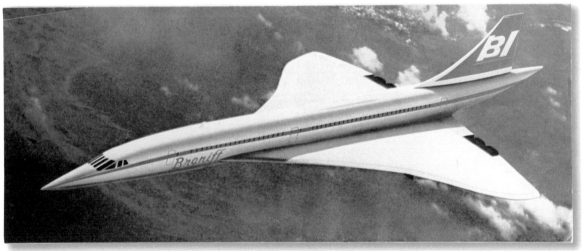

OPPOSITE and THIS PAGE
Braniff International Concorde
service timetable, 1979

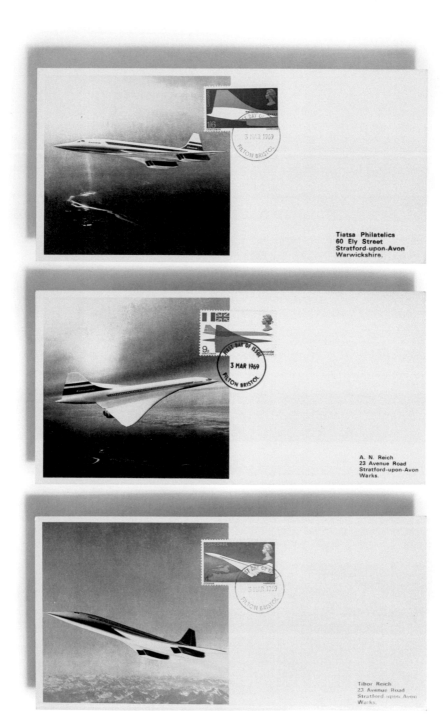

Tiatsa Philatelics
60 Ely Street
Stratford-upon-Avon
Warwickshire.

A. N. Reich
23 Avenue Road
Stratford-upon-Avon
Warks.

Tibor Reich
23 Avenue Road
Stratford-upon-Avon
Warks.

CONCORDE

flight into the future

The story of the
British and French
technical achievement
in building Concorde
- a new dimension in air travel

BUILDING

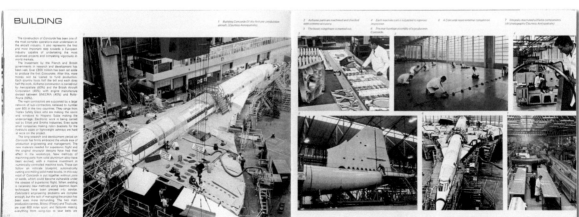

3 | LIFESTYLE: THE DESIGNERS
1960-81

The success of a commercial airliner is greatly dependent on the quality of its hospitality, and in that regard, Concorde quickly set the highest bar.

Concorde 001, the first of two prototypes constructed after the 1962 treaty between France and Britain, made its maiden test flight on March 2, 1969. Two years later it embarked on its first transatlantic flight as part of a sales and demonstration tour. In June 1972 Concorde 002 began a tour of the Middle and Far East. The stunning crash of the Soviet supersonic Tupolev Tu-144 at the 1973 Paris Air Show immediately following a successful Concorde demonstration dampened public enthusiasm for commercial supersonic travel, but nevertheless Concorde officially took to the skies in 1976.

Though economic, environmental, and thus political objections continued to surface throughout the course of Concorde's history, the undisputed brilliance of its technological innovation may have justified its aerial tenaciousness. The interior cabin design, however, was, if not an afterthought, at best a secondary concern. Aeronautically speaking, physics came before pleasure. But the success of a commercial airliner is also greatly dependent on the quality of its hospitality, and in that regard, Concorde quickly set the highest bar both literally and figuratively. Along with the evolving visual identities of Air France and British Airways, the entire Concorde package—echoing Eero Saarinen's design approach to the TWA Terminal—pioneered what was to become the art of branding.

OPPOSITE
British Airways Concorde cabin
crew uniform designed by
Sir Edwin Hardy Amies, 1976

RIGHT
Image from Concorde brochure
designed by SYNELOG and
printed in 1975, offered to passengers of the first commercial
flight, January 1976

That Concorde was a source of national pride for both Britain and France was reflected in their respective approaches to its visual design, advertising, and overall passenger experience. Air France was the first to hire an outside designer to translate Concorde's technological marvel into an equivalent brand identity. For this they turned to Raymond Loewy, a legend of industrial design known as the "Father of Streamlining," among other glowing epithets. Examples of his iconic work include the Shell logo, the Studebaker Avanti, the Air Force One livery, industrial design and graphic design for numerous passenger loco-motive lines, and, later, NASA's Skylab. Clearly Loewy was the man for the job, but he was also perhaps inspired by the physical limitations of the design brief to create an interior cabin experience significantly more sophisticated than that of the British Concordes.

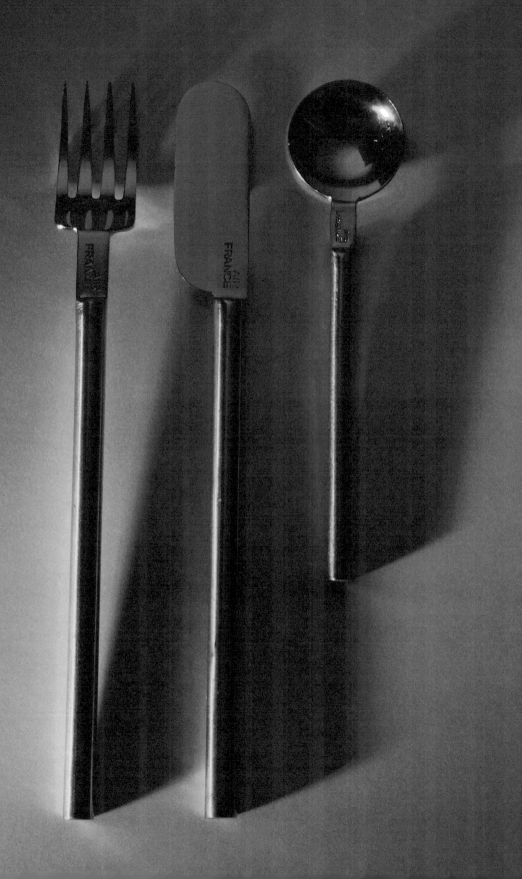

Andy Warhol made it a point of pride to steal the Raymond Loewy flatware, encouraging others to do so "because it was a collectible."

The most iconic design from Loewy's Air France Concorde remains the stainless steel Christofle flatware. Each piece is individually engraved "Air France" and the uniformly long stems, sometimes sleeved in formal black or white, mirror Concorde's exaggerated length. The lollipop shape of the spoon and the paddle-like knife add a note of charming whimsy to the design's minimal elegance. It must have been nigh impossible to return the cutlery to the flight attendants, and in fact, appropriating "prezzies" during one's flight became one of Concorde's unofficial perks.[9] None other than tastemaker Andy Warhol made it a point of pride to steal the Loewy flatware, encouraging others to do so "because it was a collectible."[10]

From the china service to the latches of the seat-back tables to the meal trays to the geometry of the headrests, the modern, forward-thinking stylings of Loewy further elevated what had become one of travel's most rarefied experiences. There was also a sense of play and brightness—most notably in the colored fabric seat covers—to offset what could have felt cramped and claustrophobic had flight times been longer. The design extended into the reception area at Paris's Charles de Gaulle Airport, which Loewy furnished with Le Corbusier chairs. But the design element Loewy was said to be most pleased with was his ceiling treatment—a black band that ran the length of the two cabins, creating the illusion of greater width.[11]

OPPOSITE
Air France Concorde Raymond
Loewy stainless steel flatware,
c. 1970s

ABOVE
Air France Concorde matchbook,
c. 1970s

Passengers were constantly
reminded that they were comfortably
ensconced in the lap of luxury.

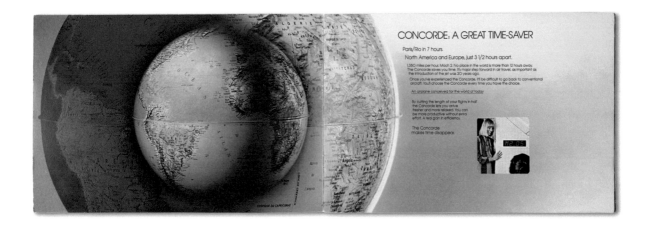

CONCORDE: A GREAT TIME-SAVER

Paris/Rio in 7 hours.

North America and Europe, just 3 1/2 hours apart.

1,350 miles per hour. Mach 2. No place in the world is more than 12 hours away. The Concorde saves you time. It's major step forward in air travel, as important as the introduction of the jet was 20 years ago.

Once you've experienced the Concorde, it'll be difficult to go back to conventional aircraft. You'll choose the Concorde every time you have the choice.

An airplane conceived for the world of today.

By cutting the length of your flights in half the Concorde lets you arrive fresher and more relaxed. You can be more productive without extra effort. A real gain in efficiency.

The Concorde makes time disappear.

**OPPOSITE, THIS PAGE,
and FOLLOWING PAGES**
Concorde brochure designed
by SYNELOG and printed in
1975, offered to passengers
of the first commercial flight,
January 1976

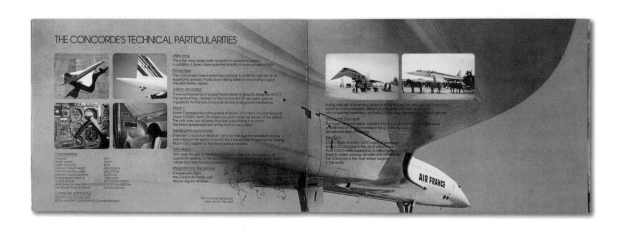

THE CONCORDE'S TECHNICAL PARTICULARITIES

Delta wing
This is the wing design best adapted to supersonic speed. In addition, it gives unprecedented stability in every phase of flight.

Droop nose
The Concorde's nose is extremely pointed, to knife through the air at supersonic speeds. It folds down during takeoff and landing to give the pilot better visibility.

Exterior decoration
It was conceived by a young French team of graphic designers, RCA 2. The symbol they created for the Concorde's fin has been used as a guide to Air France's Concorde service in all ground installations.

Mach 2
Mach 1 corresponds to the speed of sound (675 mph). You'll be flying at Mach 2 (1350 mph). On board you won't even be aware of the speed. The only way you will know how fast you're flying is to watch the Mach speed indicator at the front of your cabin.

Breaking the sound barrier
There isn't a sound or vibration, not even the slightest sensation, as you pass beyond the speed of sound. You'll know when it happens by seeing Mach 1.00 register on the Mach speed indicator.

Sonic Boom
Only over the sea or deserted terrain does the Concorde fly at supersonic speeds. So the sonic boom it leaves behind doesn't create any disturbance whatsoever.

Integration into the airlines
In supersonic flight, the Concorde travels well above regular airlines.

During take off and landing, when it is flying at subsonic altitudes, the Concorde's extreme maneuverability allows it to integrate with normal air traffic without special treatment, and without disturbing the passengers in other aircraft.

Flying the Concorde
The many present airline captains who have piloted the Concorde have already not only an impressive flying ability but also a remarkable ease of piloting.

Test flights
2,500 flights of which 1,500 were with passengers: 5,500 hours in the air of which more than 2,000 were supersonic. 6 million miles flown in widely varying climates and conditions, the Concorde is the most tested airplane in the world.

Characteristics

Wingspan 84 ft
Length overall 204 ft
Height (on entry) 40 ft
Maximum takeoff weight 400,000 lb
Maximum landing weight 245,000 lb
Maximum cruising altitude 3,500 m/h
Cruising speed Mach 2
Cruising altitude 60,000 ft
4 engines Olympus 593 (RR) ROLLS ROYCE
Individual power at takeoff 34,000 pounds

Conceived and built by
AÉROSPATIALE (France) and
BRITISH AIRCRAFT CORPORATION (Grande-Bretagne)

The Concorde has already been all over the world.

AIR FRANCE

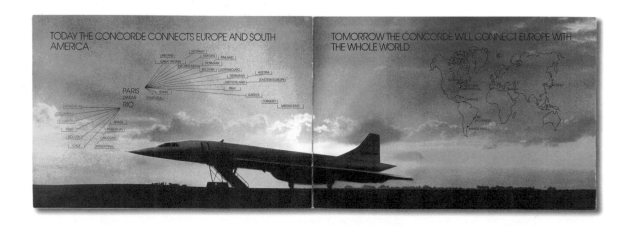

TODAY THE CONCORDE CONNECTS EUROPE AND SOUTH AMERICA

IRELAND
GREAT BRITAIN
NETHERLANDS
NORWAY
SWEDEN FINLAND
DENMARK
BELGIUM LUXEMBOURG
GERMANY
SWITZERLAND
ITALY
SPAIN
PORTUGAL
AUSTRIA
EASTERN EUROPE
GREECE
TURKEY
MIDDLE-EAST

PARIS
DAKAR
RIO

VENEZUELA
COLUMBIA
ECUADOR
PERU
BOLIVIA
CHILE
BRAZIL
PARAGUAY
URUGUAY
ARGENTINA

TOMORROW THE CONCORDE WILL CONNECT EUROPE WITH THE WHOLE WORLD

THE PEACEFUL AMBIANCE OF AN ULTRA-FAST FLIGHT

The Concorde's interior has been perfectly adapted to supersonic flight. The cabin is long and streamlined but the originality of the seats — high backs with wrap-around headrests — creates the impression of a series of separate compartments. It's as if the people at your side were the only passengers on the plane.

The interior design by CEI - Raymond Loewy, is a warm harmony of tans and brown, brightened by a touch of green here and there. In the brilliance of high altitudes, the cabin has a kind of elegance that's discreet and cheerful at the same time.

Naturally the Concorde also provides all the traditional elements of comfort on board: individual reading lights, adjustable air vents, reclining seats. As well as a music selector that lets you choose from 7 programs, including 3 stereo.

100 passengers, first class, divided into two cabins of 40 and 60 seats.

CONCORDE: A NEW WORLD OF FLYING

1,350 MILES PER HOUR, MACH 2

What will surprise you most throughout your flight on the Concorde is that you won't have the slightest indication of its incredible speed. You'll feel nothing extraordinary, neither during takeoff, passing the sound barrier, nor at supersonic speed.

The Concorde's unique delta wing gives the plane unprecedented stability. Flying is so smooth, so imperceptible, that all you'll retain after traveling thousands of miles is the memory of several enjoyable, relaxing hours.

cabin baggage
M199

British
airways

name

flight number

British
airways Concorde

OPPOSITE
British Airways Concorde
luggage tag in original
graphic identity, c. 1970s

ABOVE
British Airways Concorde crew
member and the bulkhead
Machmeter, 1977

The sense of the new and modern that Loewy championed was further reinforced in the Air France logo and wordmark, created by influential French typographer and designer Roger Excoffon (1910–1983). A customized variation of Excoffon's Antique Olive typeface marked the liveries of Air France Concorde and all its promotional and supplementary materials. Though Excoffon intended the Antique Olive typeface to rival the ubiquitous Helvetica, it was deemed to have too much character to be widely adopted outside of France, which is precisely why it succeeded so well in distinguishing the Air France brand identity.

While the first iteration of British Airways Concorde did not consult with a renowned designer, and in fact offered a traditional interior design intended to reassure passengers unaccustomed to supersonic flight, its overall brand identity was consistent and clear, trumpeting the glory days of the empire. From the plush, leather seating and the pub-like menu design to the British Airways coat of arms mounted within Concorde's capital C and the blue and gold color scheme, passengers were constantly reminded that they were comfortably ensconced in the lap

LEFT
British Airways Concorde cabin
crew uniform in navy and pale
blue with cashmere jacket, 1976

OPPOSITE, TOP
British Airways Concorde cabin
crew uniform, 1976

OPPOSITE, BOTTOM
Sir Edwin Hardy Amies, 1974

FOLLOWING PAGES
Queen Elizabeth II on Concorde
G-BOAE during the Silver
Jubilee Royal Tour of the
Caribbean, 1977

of luxury. Had the fuselage been any larger, the flight attendants might have worn the tall bearskin hats of the Queen's Guard. Fortunately the uniforms of the cabin crew reflected a more contemporary, free-flowing couture, despite being designed by Sir Edwin Hardy Amies (1909–2003), best known for being the official dressmaker of Queen Elizabeth II for several decades.

Between the technological excellence of Concorde, the privileged sense of partaking in something at the vanguard of modern experience—especially as reflected by the airliners' advertising and visual design—and the pure wonder that came with flying at twice the speed of sound above the planet's weather, establishing brand loyalty was not a problem. The goal was to maintain and expand it. For example, "when Concorde first entered service, critics were quick to point out that the equivalent of half the flight time was 'wasted' in airport procedures...With this in mind, the British Airways Concorde Brand Management Team arranged everything to cut the red tape."[12] When such attentive service preceded the jaw-dropping aspects of supersonic flight, where "at Mach 2 there's no sensation of speed at all... you almost feel that you're just hanging suspended in space, and you're waiting for Mother Earth to spin around, and your destination to arrive below you,"[13] brand identity quickly became a lifestyle.

In the last two decades of its remarkable history, fourteen Concordes transported the world's pantheon of the rich and famous. Feted on board with caviar and champagne, the head-turning Concorde club included celebrities such as Joan Collins, Sean Connery, Mick Jagger, Elton John, Annie Lenox, Luciano Pavarotti, Robert Redford, Rod Stewart, Sting and Elizabeth Taylor. Even Queen Elizabeth The Queen Mother celebrated her eighty-fifth birthday by enjoying a light lunch at 1,350 mph (2,172 kmh). As Maya Angelou opined, "Flying the Concorde is not only convenient, it's a kind of social circumstance, which makes for a club group. So those who fly the Concorde are Concorders. And somehow you smile a little more at people on the plane, and get smiled at more frequently."[14] And to stay apace with this unique lifestyle, both British Airways and Air France would continue to refine Concorde into a new era.

OPPOSITE, TOP
Pin for the Elton John "Louder
Than Concorde (But Not Quite
As Pretty)" tour, 1976

OPPOSITE, BOTTOM
British airline entrepreneur Sir
Freddie Laker at British Airways
Concorde check-in, 1978

THIS PAGE
Mick Jagger and Bianca Jagger
board British Airways Concorde
at Heathrow Airport, 1970

check in

British Airways Concorde
check-in at Heathrow Airport, 1976

THIS PAGE
British Airways Concorde
coaster set, c. 1970s

OPPOSITE
British Airways Concorde
luggage tag in original
graphic identity, c. 1970s

British airways Concorde

Flight Certificate

By travelling on
British Airways Concorde

has joined the select
group who have travelled
at Mach II in the world's
first supersonic passenger
aircraft

Capt. B. Walpole General Manager Concorde

Concorde

Concorde

Concorde
A Supersonic Success Story

Since its inaugural flight on 21st January 1976, more than three quarters of a million passengers have flown in British Airways Concorde.

Almost nine years of commercial flying, to unprecedented levels of operational excellence, have been completed. As many as thirty-four Concorde flights cross the Atlantic, between London, New York, Washington and Miami every week of the year.

Concorde – the intercontinental express – has established beyond question its unique contribution to the business world, where time, quite simply, is money. But for all its practicality, the fascination of this beautiful aeroplane remains. How else could you hope to travel from New York's Kennedy Airport to London Heathrow in 2 hours, 56 minutes and 35 seconds, which Concorde achieved on 1st January 1983?

Certainly few other aircraft have inspired a comparable level of enthusiastic interest.

Some of the questions most frequently asked by Concorde passengers are answered on the inside cover.

British airways

British airways

London—New York

3h55

Heritage '84 is Britain's great theme this year. Throughout the land—in cities, towns and villages —special celebrations are taking place to mark more than 1,000 years of British heritage. All are welcome to the party.

BA 193 Cen. F 26984

How will I know when supersonic speed is achieved?

Only by watching the machmeter at the front of the cabin. No sensations other than those normally felt in flight are experienced, with the exception of a tiny 'nudge' in the back which you might feel as the engine reheats are brought in to accelerate towards Mach 1—not unlike the sensation of an automatic car changing gear.

What speeds do Mach numbers indicate?

Mach 1 = the speed of sound. At typical Concorde cruising altitudes this is approximately 670 miles per hour (1,075 kilometres per hour). Mach 1.5 = 1,000 mph (1,610 km/h) Mach 2 = twice the speed of sound, and Concorde's cruising speed at a height of 55,000 ft, approximately 1,340 mph (2,150 km/h).

Why does Concorde have a 'droop nose'?

The long aerodynamic shape of Concorde's nose must be altered to allow greater visibility to the pilot during take-off and landing.

Why are the windows smaller than in subsonic aircraft?

Concorde's design could have featured larger windows, but various international requirements precluded this.

Why is the sky darker at Concorde's cruising height?

The familiar blue of the sky is caused by the scattering effect of the earth's atmosphere on the light from the sun. With altitude the atmosphere becomes thinner, so the scattering is lessened. Hence astronauts observe a 'black sky' in space. From Concorde's cruising height you can also see clearly the curvature of the earth.

Some more Concorde facts and figures:

Overall length: 204 feet (62.2m)
Wingspan: 84 feet (25.5m)
Overall height: 37 feet (11.3m)
Engines: 4 Rolls-Royce/Snecma Olympus 593-610 turbojets with reheat
Take-off thrust: 4 x 169kN — 38 000 lbf (17 240 kg)
Cruise thrust: 4 x 30.25 kN — 6 800 lbf (3 085 kg)
Cruising speed: Mach 2 — 1 340 mph (2 150 km/h) approx.

Cruising altitude: 55 000 — 60 000 feet (16 800 — 18 300 m)
Equivalent cabin altitude 5 500 feet (1 680 m)
Seating configuration: 100 'Supersonic class' seats

Designed and built jointly by British Aerospace and Aérospatiale, Bristol and Toulouse.

BA 716C

Aperitifs and Cocktails

Sweet and Dry Vermouth
Campari Soda
Americano . Negroni
Medium Dry Sherry
Dry Martini . Gin . Vodka
Bloody Mary . Old Fashioned . Manhattan
Sours – *Whisky . Gin . Brandy*
Gin Fizz

Highballs – *Whisky . Brandy . Gin . Rum*

Champagne Cocktail

Spirits

Whisky – *Scotch . Bourbon . Rye*
Gin
Vodka

Beers

Ale . Lager

Selection of Soft Drinks

Wines

Champagne
Laurent—Perrier Grand Siécle
*Presented in a bottle of unique shape used in the time of the reign of Louis XIV of
France, this classic blend of three selected vintages of Champagne epitomizes
perfection. The Champagnes are selected from the best growths of the Montagne
des Reims and the Côtes des Blancs.*

Red Bordeaux
Château Gruaud Larose 1976—St. Julien
*Château Gruaud Larose is a leading second growth château of St. Julien and
with 77 hectares under vine is one of the largest vineyards in this commune. It
constantly produces a powerful wine of great character and longevity. 1976 was a
very good year producing wines of style and elegance.*

White Burgundy
Puligny Montrachet 1982
*Full bodied, dry and perfectly mature for drinking, this Puligny Montrachet
comes from the village famous for producing two of the world's great white wines
Le Montrachet and Chevalier Montrachet.*

Liqueurs

Remy Martin Napoleon Brandy
Drambuie . Cointreau . Coffee Liqueur
Fonseca Bin 27 Port

Jamaica Macanudo cigars

Aperitifs — Champagne

Canapés
Caviar barquette, smoked salmon and goats cheese with walnuts

Lunch
Déjeuner

Terrine de foie gras et ris de veau
*A delicate terrine of goose liver and veal sweetbreads garnished with
leeks, button mushrooms and artichoke hearts marinated in olive oil,
dressed on oak leaf lettuce*

— ∗ —

Tournedos Richmond
*Tender fillet steak, pan-fried in butter, garnished with morels and
truffle, served with madeira sauce, glazed carrots, stuffed courgette
and lorette potatoes*

Suprême de tétras aux canneberges
*Braised breasts of young grouse finished in rich port wine-flavoured
sauce and garnished with cranberries
An accompaniment of glazed carrots, stuffed courgette
and lorette potatoes, completes this seasonal speciality*

Assiette froide du pêcheur
*New to Concorde, an exquisite cold plate consisting of fresh
brook trout stuffed with avocado, smoked trout and smoked salmon,
complemented by a garnish of caviar, shrimps and lobster claw
decorated with sprigs of fresh dill and lemon crown*

— ∗ —

Salade composée
Mixed salad in season, served with vinaigrette dressing

— ∗ —

Choix de fromage
*A selection of French Coulommiers, English Stilton
and Cheddar cheese*

— ∗ —

Pêche pochée au Champagne
*A fresh peach poached in pure Champagne, flavoured with vanilla
and served on a bed of strawberry mousse
Garnished with a leaf of fresh mint*

— ∗ —

Café . Café sans caféine
*Coffee or caffeine free coffee,
served with a selection of home made chocolates*

ABOVE
British Airways Concorde
Royal Doulton bone china bowl,
c. 1970s

OPPOSITE
Lunch on board British Airways
Concorde, 1976

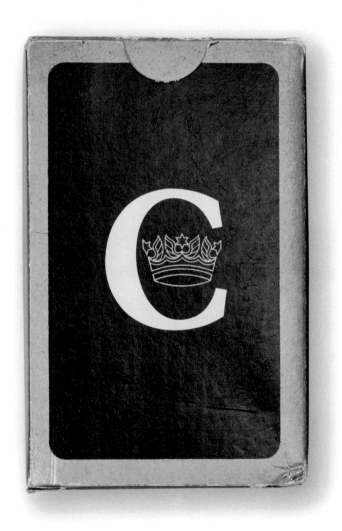

OPPOSITE
British Airways Concorde playing
cards in original graphic identity,
c. 1970s

ABOVE
Packaging for the Concorde Game
depicting British Airways Concorde
in the original livery, 1976

ABOVE
Queen Elizabeth II and Prince
Philip arrive in Saudi Arabia
on Concorde, escorted by King
Khalid for the state visit to
Riyadh, 1979

OPPOSITE
British Airways Concorde
stationery envelope in original
graphic identity, 1976

When such attentive service preceded
the jaw-dropping aspects of supersonic flight,
brand identity quickly became a lifestyle.

THIS PAGE
British Airways Concorde
stationery and envelope in
original graphic identity,
c. 1970s

OPPOSITE
British Airways Concorde
matchbox in original
graphic identity, c. 1970s

THIS PAGE
Air France Concorde
cigarette lighter, c. 1970s

OPPOSITE
Air France Concorde Cognac
Otard silver-plated hip flask,
c. 1970s

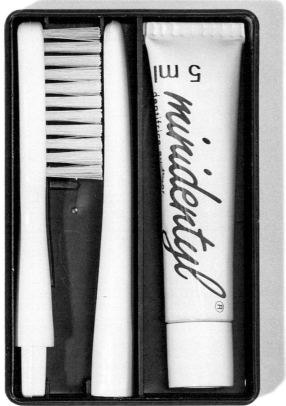

OPPOSITE
Air France Concorde Stylshave
and Stylbrush kit, c. 1970s

ABOVE
Air France Concorde
toothbrush travel kit, c. 1970s

AIR FRANCE

RÉSEAU
AMÉRIQUE DU SUD

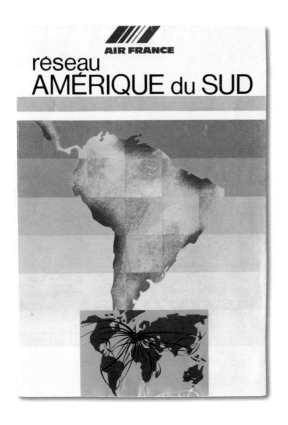

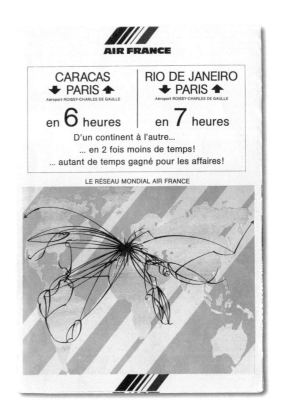

The French Revolution

The Concorde is only one part of the story.

The French are changing the way man flies.

The most advanced airplane in the world. The Concorde, flying at twice the speed of sound, is one of the most important breakthroughs in the history of commercial aviation.

Its incredible speed has cut the world in half for air travelers, and greatly reduced the effects of travel fatigue.

But the Air France Concorde is just the most obvious evidence of how France is revolutionizing commercial aviation as we know it today.

The most advanced airport in the world. It took French technology to build the most exciting airport anywhere— Charles de Gaulle. Arriving at de Gaulle is like stepping into tomorrow.

The architecture dazzles the eye. Gleaming glass tubes with moving floors transport travelers effortlessly from one area to another. There's drive-in baggage checking. An entire level of fine restaurants, bars and smart shops. Everything marvelously designed for comfort and convenience.

Life can be exquisite, even at 30,000 feet. It was Air France who took great French chefs from great French restaurants and put them into the airline business, presiding over every detail of our dining service. So instead of "airline food," we present classic gourmet cuisine aloft. And you enjoy delicacies like *Médaillon de Langouste* and *Tournedos Sauté au Poivre Vert.* That's in Tourist. In First Class, you'll

discover such sumptuous fare as *Médaillon de Foie Gras en brioche,* caviar from Iran, Lobster *Parisienne,* and Rack of Lamb *Provençal.*

And, of course, incredible *vins de France*—from one of the greatest cellars in the world.

Air travel has changed dramatically. And nobody has done more to change it than we have.

France. A nation in love with the air.

AIR FRANCE

Today, aviation history is being written in French.

Le Chef-d'œuvre.

The masterpiece. In man's centuries-old pursuit of the skies, supersonic flight is his loftiest achievement. A breathtaking aerodynamic machine, Concorde soars at twice the speed of sound, reduces flight times by half, and creates a whole new sensory experience in the air.

Air France proudly pilots the most tested, most researched, most beautiful aircraft in history. Our Concorde network now spans from Paris to Caracas, Rio de Janeiro and Washington D.C.

Air France brings you the masterpiece of commercial aviation. The incomparable Concorde.

AIR FRANCE ////
The best of France to all the world.

OPPOSITE, TOP
Air France Concorde brochure,
c. 1970s

OPPOSITE, BOTTOM
Air France Concorde
advertisement, c. 1980s

ABOVE
Air France Concorde
advertisement, c. 1980s

L'efficacité.

Efficiency. This is the true value of Concorde. Supersonic flight literally makes the most of your time. Concorde takes you to your destination in half the time of subsonic flight, thereby affording you new productive hours. And Concorde emphatically reduces flight fatigue, assuring you of your best performance upon arrival. The Air France Concorde network now spans from Paris to New York, Washington, Dallas-Fort Worth*, Mexico City, Caracas, Dakar and Rio de Janeiro. Travel at optimum efficiency with Concorde.

AIR FRANCE ///
The best of France to all the world.

La Différence.

Concorde is just one way the French have perfected business travel.

The Gallic passion for good living becomes a beautiful asset to business travelers on Air France.

Concorde. Ah, the heady pleasure of easing across the Atlantic at Mach 2! You arrive in Paris in half the time, virtually as fresh as when you started.

747 First Class. The exquisite Air France tradition of hospitality is simply unrivaled. Brut champagne with caviar or fresh foie gras. Grand cru wines. A six-course banquet dinner, served in an atmosphere of linen and Limoges.

747 Business Class. We have created a citadel of peace and quiet for economy class passengers paying full fare—a separate cabin, plus cocktails, fine French champagne and wines, imported cheeses, cordials, in-flight entertainment, all complimentary. (Available from selected gateways.)

Choose Air France. Enjoy la différence. **AIR FRANCE** ///
The best of France to all the world.

27

La Différence.

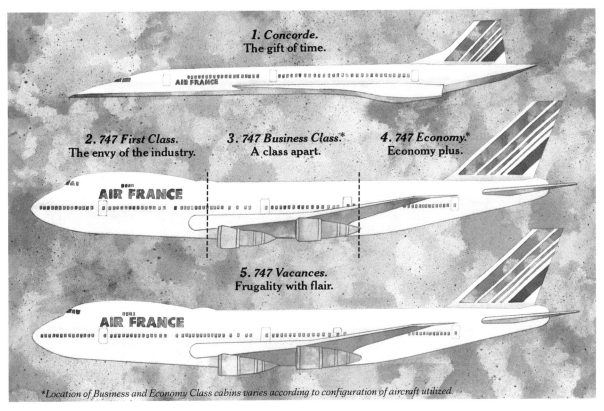

1. *Concorde.*
The gift of time.

2. *747 First Class.*
The envy of the industry.

3. *747 Business Class.*
A class apart.

4. *747 Economy.*
Economy plus.

5. *747 Vacances.*
Frugality with flair.

Location of Business and Economy Class cabins varies according to configuration of aircraft utilized.

Only one airline has 5 ways to fly to Europe. Air France.

And with more ways than any other airline, it's more likely you'll find an Air France class perfectly suited to your needs.

Concorde. The gift of time. Fly at twice the speed of sound, and arrive in Paris virtually as fresh as when you left America.

747 First Class. The envy of the industry, and one of the great experiences of air travel. Once accustomed to our style, you won't want to settle for anything less.

747 Business Class. A class apart. Check-in, boarding and cabin are all separate. Cuisine à la Business Class includes champagne, fine wines and cognac. Flights from New York, Chicago, Houston and soon from Los Angeles.

747 Economy. A variety of convenient flights and budget fares with a touch of class.

747 Vacances. Even when the French are frugal, they do it in style. The lowest scheduled fare to Paris, and the entire plane is devoted to Vacances travelers. Available from New York during peak season.

Choose Air France for *la différence.* More ways to get there, and each with its own unique features.

AIR FRANCE ////
The best of France to all the world.

TOP
British Airways Concorde
in Singapore, 1974

BOTTOM
British Airways Concorde
G-BOAD in Singapore
Airlines livery, 1976

OPPOSITE
British Airways Concorde
G-N94AD in Singapore
Airlines livery, 1977

4 | THE NEW LOOK: DESIGN DIVERSITY

1982-2003

If the gods needed a plane,
Concorde was the way to go.

Thanks to shrewd overpricing, Concorde operations began to turn a profit during the mid-1980s. By then the Concorde lifestyle had also risen to the occasion, mirroring its exquisite exterior. As Maya Angelou noted, all you had to do was look around (at least after cigar smoking had been banned) to appreciate the elevated surroundings. If the gods needed a plane, Concorde was the way to go.

Fittingly, Concorde passengers dined like gods. The carefully curated menus were a far cry from today's prepackaged, boxed meals. From foie gras to caviar to lobster, the food was real, high-end, and intensely flavored to counteract taste buds dampened by the dryness of the pressurized cabin. To that end, British Airways also maintained the Concorde Cellar,

a selection of wine, champagne, and port to stock each flight. By the time the seat-back tables had been cleared, passengers would be preparing for landing—as if they had entered a fine dining establishment in London and exited to find themselves on the streets of New York.

While Air France was the first to implement a sophisticated level of design into the Concorde experience by consulting a known designer, British Airways quickly made up ground, especially after its first tentative steps. On December 4, 1984, a new logo, livery, and brand identity were unveiled. Developed by American design firm Landor Associates (a minor controversy, as it was standard at the time for British companies to contract British design firms), the

new look transformed the brand into a model of sophistication and luxury. The color scheme—pearl gray, midnight blue, and brilliant red—pointed toward a refined elegance lacking in the traditional pomp and circumstance of the original palette. Curves and serifs had been dropped from the typeface, and its cleaner, angular, all caps makeover reflected a bolder, more modern entity appropriate for the Concorde lifestyle and its futuristic fuselage. Even the British Airways coat of arms had been streamlined into a monochromatic cutout stamped onto the midnight-blue tail over the Union Jack. The most radical and distinctive change was the redesign of the blue "speedbird" toward the nose of the craft into the red "speedwing" running the length of the fuselage, as well as under all recurrences of the British Airways logo.

As successful as the Landor livery was, British Airways continually refined and upgraded the overall brand in the ensuing years, though not all the changes were universally applauded. Cabin interior upgrades like new leather seats, leather

As if they had entered a fine
dining establishment in London
and exited to find themselves
on the streets of New York.

OPPOSITE
British Airways Concorde
ticket jacket in Landor
Associates speedwing identity,
c. 1980s

ABOVE
British Airways Concorde
crew members Sue Higton
and Maggie Andrews attending
to passengers; cabin in Landor
Associates speedwing
interior design, 1986

135

The passengers who fly aboard Concorde are experienced and discriminating travellers. They are judges of excellence. For them, therefore, we have a simple aim. It is to offer the finest cabin service in the world. Friendly, unobtrusive, and very British. The men and women who serve aboard Concorde are proud of their skills. They take a pride in the standard of service they offer you. They are professionals, trained to know when you need attention, and equally important, when you don't. If you would like a drink, or a

magazine, or something as simple as an eyelid shade, you only have to ask. If you would rather be left alone with a company report, a book or just your own thoughts, you will find that Concorde suits your mood remarkably well. Your cabin crew will recognise it and respect it. Whether it's your first supersonic flight or your fiftieth, a transatlantic crossing by Concorde will always be a very special experience. We want you to enjoy it.

A Concorde flight is an experience to be savoured. Elegance blended with exquisite standards are in keeping with the occasion. On a typical Concorde Atlantic crossing, you'll be served either a morning meal, lunch or dinner, depending on the time of day. Delicate canapés accompanied by fine champagne precede a meal selection designed by our own award winning chefs, in association with some of the world's culinary masters. Light and appetising creations blended with internationally recognised favourites provide a meal unparalleled in the air. A typical lunch might begin with a specially selected melon combined with seasonal fresh fruits or a plate of the finest new season's Scottish salmon. The choice of main course might include a prime grilled

filet Angus beef, or a delicious lobster creation. Particular importance is paid to the needs of business or health conscious travellers who might prefer a lighter main course or even a selection of delicious cold meals. Of course, vegetarian or kosher meals receive the same creative attention. To complement fine food we seek out choice growths from some of the greatest vineyards in Europe. We know that to do justice to a fine meal served in the very special ambience of Concorde, wines must be chosen with professionalism and care. Classical champagnes, renowned clarets and distinguished Burgundies rub shoulders with the finest port and liqueurs. Concorde. For people with a taste for the good things of life.

OPPOSITE
British Airways Concorde
brochure in Landor Associates
speedwing identity, c. 1980s

ABOVE
British Airways Concorde
opera glasses and case
in Landor Associates
speedwing identity, c. 1980s

ABOVE
British Airways Concorde
refurbishment with new seats,
overhead lockers, and lighting,
June 1993

OPPOSITE
British Airways Concorde
wallet in Landor Associates
speedwing identity, c. 1980s

covers on the bulkheads, larger overhead bins, new galleys, and improved toilets were in line with passengers' lofty expectations, but the replacement of the iconic Marilake Aero Systems cabin display was roundly decried. In 1997 British design agency Newell & Sorrell gave the British Airways brand yet another overhaul, moving away from a perceived stuffiness toward a more open, global perspective. Jettisoned were the coat of arms, the red "speedwing," and the Union Jack. The "speedwing" was replaced with a new ribbon symbol called the "speedmarque" near the nose of the fuselage. The colors of the Union Jack remained on the tail in the form of a fluttering banner. And the typeface was softened and given a uniform x-height for all letters, suggesting Britain's more egalitarian status in the world.

Air France further refined Loewy's interior designs, most notably in the mid-1980s when architect and decorator Pierre Gautier-Delaye (1923–2006) (an alumnus of Loewy's Paris studio) updated the interior cabin with a tulip red, blue, and beige stripe. (Air France justifiably never felt the need to improve its Excoffon logo design during Concorde's

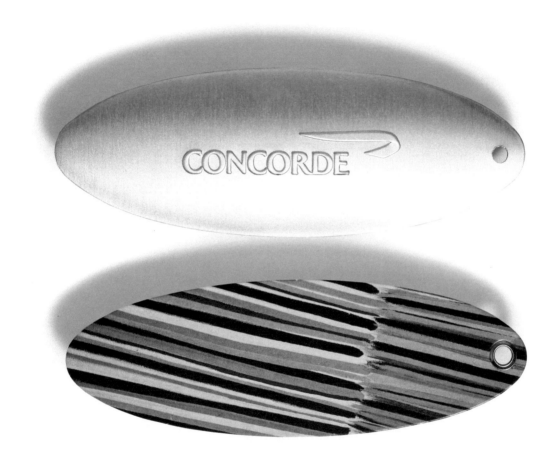

OPPOSITE
British Airways Concorde
in Newell & Sorrell
speedmarque livery, 1997

ABOVE
British Airways Concorde
luggage tags in Newell &
Sorrell speedmarque identity,
c. 1990s

FOLLOWING PAGES
British Airways Concorde
room at John F. Kennedy
International Airport with
BAW002 in Newell & Sorrell
speedmarque livery on tarmac,
2003

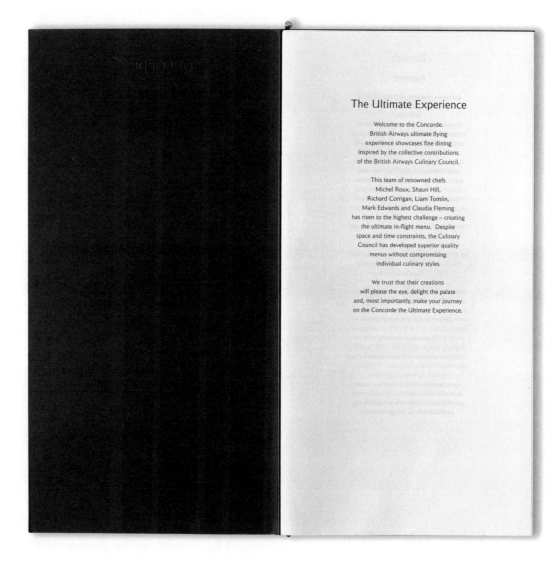

The Ultimate Experience

Welcome to the Concorde.
British Airways ultimate flying
experience showcases fine dining
inspired by the collective contributions
of the British Airways Culinary Council.

This team of renowned chefs
Michel Roux, Shaun Hill,
Richard Corrigan, Liam Tomlin,
Mark Edwards and Claudia Fleming
has risen to the highest challenge – creating
the ultimate in-flight menu. Despite
space and time constraints, the Culinary
Council has developed superior quality
menus without compromising
individual culinary styles

We trust that their creations
will please the eye, delight the palate
and, most importantly, make your journey
on the Concorde the Ultimate Experience.

OPPOSITE
British Airways Concorde
ticket jacket in Newell & Sorrell
speedmarque identity, c. 1990s

ABOVE
British Airways Concorde
Anya Hindmarch pouch in Newell
& Sorrell speedmarque identity,
c. 1990s

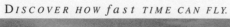

twenty-seven years of service.) In the 1990s, to commemorate Concorde's twentieth anniversary, French designer Andrée Putman (1925–2013) brought her touch to the Air France cabin treatment after winning a design competition that included Philippe Starck, Philippe Boisselier, and Gautier-Delaye. Even before the competition, Putman had accumulated a mental list of improvements as a frequent traveler on the Paris–New York service. She "wanted to change everything" and "disliked the luggage racks, the colors, the shape of the seats."[15] But when her redesign was unveiled, passengers may have been surprised by her restraint. The seats exhibited the most distinctive transformation—they were higher, with rounded headrests covered antimacassar-like in white cotton that, according to Putman, referenced the classic French children's book character Babar the Elephant. The other notable change occurred in the gray, navy blue, and beige carpeting patterned with a geometric frieze. Elsewhere, Putman's improvements were in the details, from the beige linen napkins to the immaculate white china streaked with a blue New York skyline.

Toward the end of the twentieth century, engineers at British Airways realized their fleet of seven Concordes was fit enough to fly for at least a decade or more. But while the exterior remained as futuristic as ever, the interior showed signs of age, and in 1999 Factorydesign, working with British design guru Sir Terence Conran, was commissioned to bring the interior experience up to speed. While the premature grounding of Concorde in 2003 prevented the full implementation of Conran's vision, the completed elements brilliantly showcased his design savvy. As Conran explained, "We wanted to create an interior that was as light and elegant as the exterior, and a feeling of comfort and luxury... We selected chairs that took inspiration from my idols, Charles and Ray Eames—they were ink-blue Connolly leather with a cradle mechanism, footrest, and contoured headrest for comfort and support. We also wanted to make the interior of the passenger cabin brighter with different lighting, which would change to a cool-blue wash throughout the cabin when the Concorde flew through the sound barrier at Mach 1—that would have been a wonderful sight."[16]

Air France Concorde crew
members in Andrée Putman-
designed cabin of Concorde
F-BVFA, Roissy, France, 2003

ABOVE
Air France Concorde cabin
designed by Andrée Putman,
2003

OPPOSITE
Air France Concorde logo on
seat belt latch, 2003

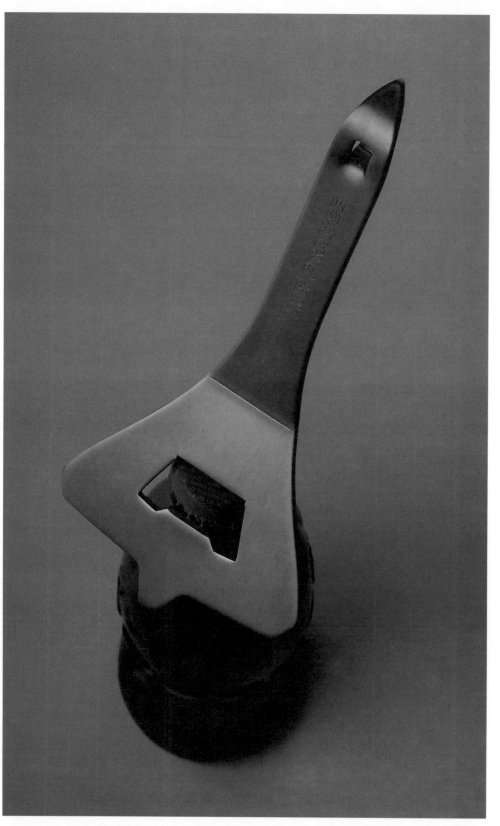

AFRICA

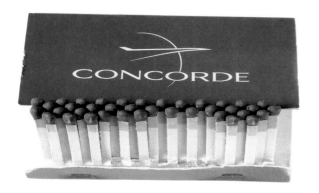

CONCORDE

THE FINE ART
OF BEING UNIQUE

CONCORDE

CONCORDE, THE SHORTEST PATH BETWEEN EUROPE AND THE UNITED STATES. PARIS IS NOW ONLY 3 HOURS AND 45 MINUTES FROM NEW YORK. EVERY DAY AIR FRANCE INVITES YOU TO GO BACK IN TIME. TAKE OFF FROM PARIS AT 11 A.M. AND ARRIVE IN NEW YORK AT 8:45 A.M. WITH CONCORDE, YOU ENJOY THE UNIQUE EXPERIENCE OF REACHING YOUR DESTINATION BEFORE YOU HAVE EVEN LEFT! FLYING WITH CONCORDE ALSO REDUCES THE EFFECTS OF JET LAG. ON YOUR RETURN TO PARIS FROM NEW YORK, YOU GET IN AT 10:45 P.M., IN TIME FOR A FULL NIGHT'S SLEEP. FAR ABOVE THE NORMAL FLIGHT PATHS, AT AN ALTITUDE OF 59,000 FEET, CONCORDE ENTERS INTO ITS OWN REALM WHERE NOTHING HINDERS ITS FLIGHT. IT ATTAINS ITS CRUISING SPEED, MACH 2, AT THIS ALTITUDE. FLYING THE FASTEST JET IN THE WORLD GIVES YOU THE SMOOTHEST OF FLIGHTS. THIS IS BECAUSE CONCORDE KNOWS NO TURBULENCE IN THE DEEP BLUE STRATOSPHERE.

OUR ONLY STANDARD IS EXCELLENCE

On the ground and in the air, Concorde staff take care of each tiny detail of your trip. The more you fly Concorde, the better we know you, and the better we can anticipate your needs.

BE IT IN PARIS OR NEW YORK

In both Paris-Charles de Gaulle 2 and JFK, check in at the counters reserved only for you and enjoy the private lounges. Thanks to our perso-nalized coat-check service, you can cross the short distance separating you from the aircraft with your hands as free as your mind.

ON BOARD, A NEW DECOR TO ENHANCE YOUR WELL-BEING

Andrée Putman's new decor gives preference to rounded forms, discreet restful blends of colours and elegant materials. Meals on board Concorde are a happy mix of French culinary classics and inventive new recipes. The menu is always the work

of a great chef and contains a choice of six superb vintages including two champagnes. Specially-designed porcelain tableware, Christofle cutlery, linen table cloth and napkins all contribute to the discreetly elegant atmosphere. Thanks to the speed indicators in the cabin and the announcement from your Captain, you will know exactly when you break the sound barrier. An official certificate will commemorate your first supersonic flight.

BE IT IN NEW YORK OR IN PARIS

On your arrival, prompt delivery of your baggage and convenient Concorde schedules enable you to avoid congestion at the airport and on the highways. In one day you can leave Paris, conduct a three-hour meeting in New York and be back the same evening. At JFK, if you request it beforehand, a fully-equipped meeting room, close to the arrivals lounge, is at your disposal. If you are in transit, there are free taxi or limousine transfers between the various airports in Paris and in New York.

OPPOSITE, LEFT
Air France Concorde matchbook,
c. 1990s

OPPOSITE, RIGHT
Air France Concorde brochure,
c. 1990s

ABOVE
Air France Concorde brochure,
c. 1990s

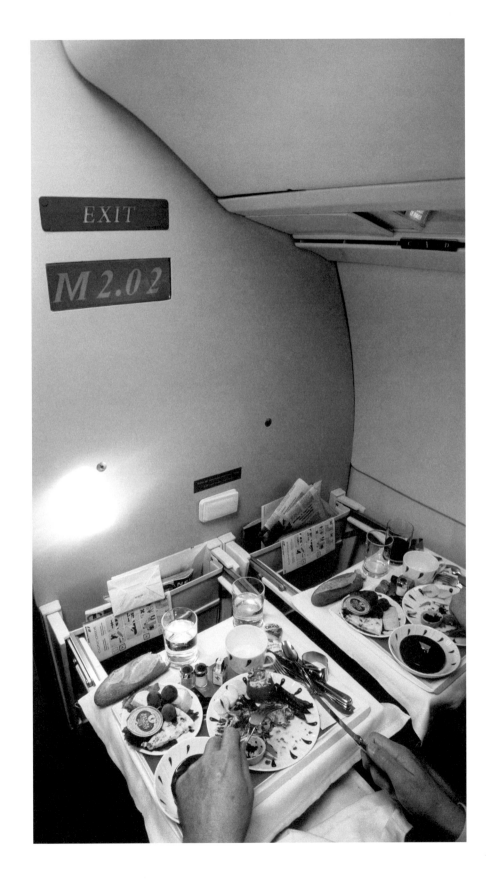

OPPOSITE
Air France Concorde
Millennium 2000 menu
designed by Jean Boggio,
2000

RIGHT
Lunch on board Air France
Concorde under the Machmeter,
c. 1990s

OPPOSITE
Air France Concorde
Millennium 2000 menu
designed by Jean Boggio,
2000

THIS PAGE
Air France Concorde
champagne bucket, c. 1990s

YOUR CONCORDE TIMETABLE TO FRANCE

CONCORDE DEPARTS NEW YORK (JFK) AT 8AM DAILY AND ARRIVES IN PARIS (CDG) AT 5:45 PM WITH SAME DAY CONNECTIONS TO OVER 40 DESTINATIONS IN EUROPE.

CONCORDE DEPARTS PARIS (CDG) AT 11AM DAILY AND ARRIVES IN NEW YORK (JFK) AT 8:45 AM (SAME DAY). CALL YOUR TRAVEL AGENT OR AIR FRANCE FOR RESERVATIONS, 1-800-237-2747.

TURN THE PLANE TOWARD A DESTINATION TO SEE WHAT TIME YOU'LL ARRIVE.

7:40PM

BIARRITZ
BORDEAUX
BREST
CLERMONT-FERRAND
LIMOGES
LORIENT
LYON
MARSEILLE
MONTPELLIER
MULHOUSE
NANTES
NICE
PAU
QUIMPER
STRASBOURG
TOULON
TOULOUSE
AVIGNON

AIR FRANCE

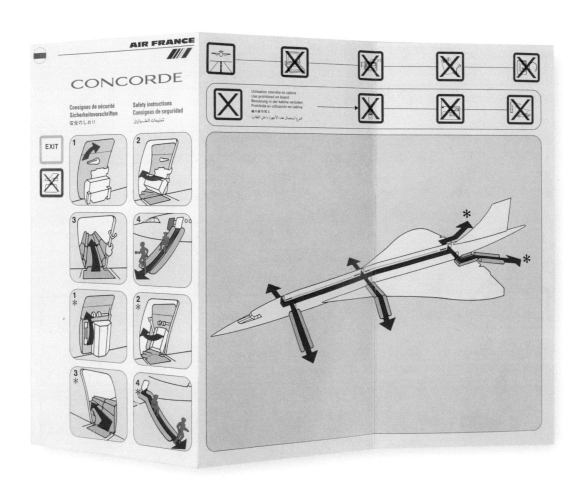

Polished aluminum armrests, spa-like bathrooms appointed with fresh flowers, brushed-steel napkin rings, Royal Doulton bone china framing light, modern fare lubricated with bottles of 1993 Puligny-Montrachet—all this invited passengers to bask in a heightened sense of style and glamour. A similar ambience pervaded Concorde lounges at Heathrow and JFK. Conran had envisioned a space that would feature the greatest furniture designers of the twentieth century—Charles (1907–1978) and Ray (1912–1988) Eames, Arne Jacobsen (1902–1971), Le Corbusier (1887–1965), Ludwig Mies van der Rohe (1886–1969)—but to his dismay, passengers voiced a preference for leather club chairs.

ABOVE and OPPOSITE
British Airways Concorde bucket seats with brushed-aluminum armrests designed by Factorydesign and Sir Terence Conran, 1999

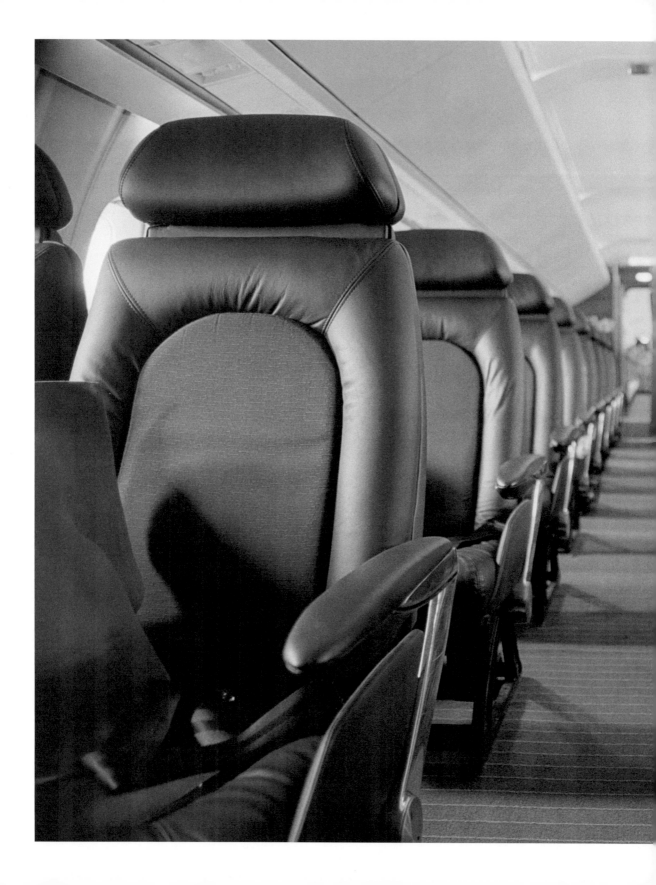

British Airways Concorde cabin
designed by Factorydesign and
Sir Terence Conran, 1999

As if life on Concordes wasn't good enough, Air France and British Airways shared a tradition of distributing parting gifts to its passengers. Not just any parting gifts, but those bearing the distinctive Concorde logo. Over the course of twenty-seven years, a unique treasure trove of Concorde tchotchkes has accumulated in the vitrines of increasingly passionate collectors, or passed hands through websites like eBay and 1stdibs. The sundry items include pens, picture frames, candlesnuffers, dopp kits, embossed leather notebooks, pill cases, flasks, lighters, and matchbooks, to name just a few. But in 2003 the magnificent era of commercial supersonic flight came to a halt. It was as if the tragic crash of Air France Flight 4590 in 2000 dealt a debilitating puncture to the unique aura of Concorde's improbable allure. Economics and safety concerns were the official reasons. The many supporters of Concorde bemoaned the lack of vision. They felt as if history had decided to regress. Time no longer equaled money. But like the timeless, graceful lines of the ubiquitous Eames lounge chair, the skies above will forever remember the flight of Concorde.

British Airways Concorde
room at John F. Kennedy
International Airport, 2003

An interior that was as light
and elegant as the exterior.

PRECEDING PAGES
British Airways Concorde
Royal Doulton bone china set,
c. 1990s

ABOVE and OPPOSITE
British Airways Concorde
bathroom designed by
Factorydesign and
Sir Terence Conran, 1999

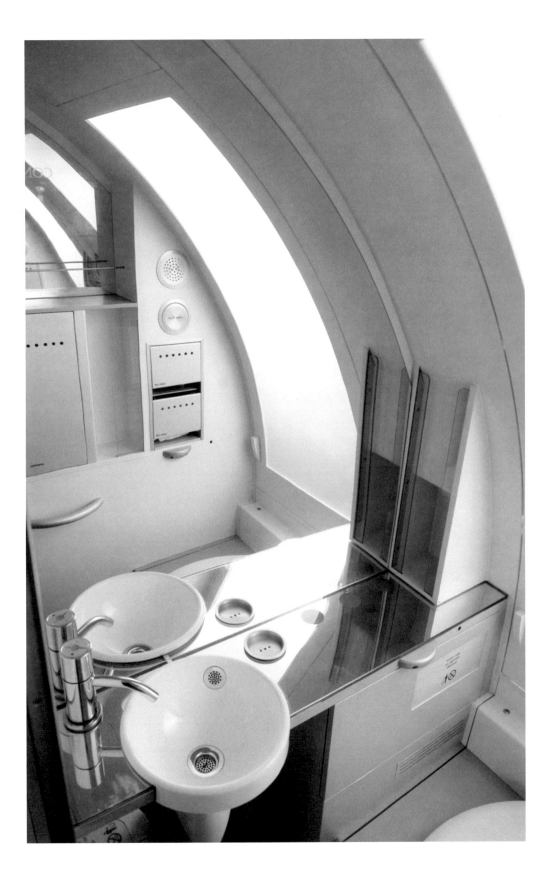

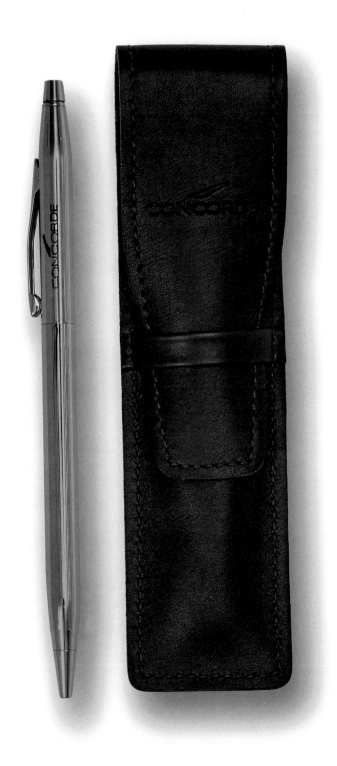

THIS PAGE
British Airways Concorde
Cross writing pen, c. 1990s

OPPOSITE
British Airways Concorde pew-
ter letter opener and paper-
weight designed by Livingstone
Trading Company, c. 1990s

OPPOSITE
Air France Concorde journal
wallet designed by
Pierre Balmain, c. 1990s

ABOVE
Air France Concorde dopp kit,
c. 1990s

The final flight,
October 24, 2003

British Airways Concorde cabin
service director Claire Sullivan
wipes away a tear, October 24, 2003

BAW002 departs John F.
Kennedy International Airport
for Heathrow Airport for the
last time, 2003

The last British Airways Concorde flight left
John F. Kennedy International Airport October 24, 2003.

AFTERWORD

Andrew Macpherson with Cindy Crawford

The Concorde's development dominated my childhood in Britain. A full decade before we ever saw it fly, its beauty and speed were often spoken of with wonder and awe. The incredible excitement it generated for myself and my classmates during its long journey to regularly scheduled service may be long forgotten today, but at the time Concorde was like a bright beacon pointing toward an incredibly glamorous and exciting future.

Russia put a man into orbit, then America put a man on the moon, but in Europe we missed out on the glory of the Space Race. Once the United States officially backed away from developing supersonic passenger travel, Concorde became a massive symbol of national pride for both us Brits and the French.

I still remember the day of its maiden voyage to Washington, DC, in the spring of 1974. We all went outside to see if we could hear it take off. Even though I was a good fifty miles to the west of Heathrow Airport, I could clearly hear those four Olympus engines powering it high into the sky. Then, around fifteen minutes later, I heard the very distant, muffled rumble of it breaking the sound barrier.

Not long after, I moved to London to start my career in photography. During those years, I was always on a motorcycle, and the only plane I could hear inside my crash helmet was Concorde. I would look up at it with a sense of pride and admiration.

As my career progressed, I moved to Paris to work as a fashion photographer, so I would see Concorde at both Heathrow and Charles de Gaulle Airport. Catching sight of it was always a special event, and today I deeply regret not photographing it on every one of those occasions, as Wolfgang Tillmans did for *Concorde*, his wonderful book of random sightings.

Though I tried on many occasions to persuade my clients it was a necessity, I sadly never got to fly on Concorde. I worked with many who did, however, so I asked supermodel Cindy Crawford to share some of her memories.

Andrew Macpherson: Concorde was such a part of the supermodel era. I remember you flying on it to jobs we did together, and of course all the to-and-fro at the time of the fashion shows. What was it like?

Cindy Crawford: It really did feel glamorous. It was like the last vestige of the golden era of travel. You'd always dress better for it because you never knew who you were going to meet. The seats weren't that big—you were definitely kind of sardined in there—but they'd bring you caviar and champagne and do everything they could to make it an incredible experience.

AM: What was it like when you'd arrive at the airport?

CC: You'd check in and wait in the first-class lounge, which was already pretty nice. But when they'd call out your flight, "Concorde flight number two to New York," or whatever it was, you really did feel special standing up and walking to the gate. Once you got on the plane, you'd always wonder who all the other passengers were, and why they were there that day. I sat next to

a lot of fascinating people, but my most fun memory was getting on the plane exhausted, falling asleep before the seat next to me was taken, and waking up an hour later to find Mick Jagger sitting next to me!

AM: What do you miss most about it?

CC: Concorde gave us the gift of time, which as a model is our most valuable commodity. Although it seemed like a luxury, it really was a necessity. I couldn't have done nearly as many jobs as I did back then without it.

AM: I really do wish I'd managed to get a ride on it, but I'd far rather have sat next to you than Mick Jagger!

ACKNOWLEDGMENTS

This survey of design and lifestyle covering a fifty-year vision that brought us the industrial and aesthetic marvel of Concorde, along with the vast ecosystem of design supporting its passenger experience, could only be realized thanks to the support of a large number of colleagues, advisors, and friends.

I am enormously thankful to Julie Muncy, my wife and partner in inspiration, who has provided astute input and encouragement throughout the entire fifteen-year life cycle of this project. Her patience, grace, support, and perspective have made possible this dream of contributing to society through inspiration and creativity.

I am deeply grateful to my mother, Gail Azerrad, who has always supported my interest in the arts. Thank you especially for the gifts of Concorde ephemera over the years.

I extend my deep thanks to Frankie Hamersma, a true pillar of support at my design studio LADdesign. Frankie's consummate attention to detail, creative spirit, and dedication have made for a wonderful collaboration in all the projects we are fortunate to work on at LADdesign, especially this passion project.

It has been an honor to consult with my dear friend and great resource Louise Sandhaus. Louise's generosity in sharing her wise experience and perspective in authoring design books of value consistently helped lead this project to realization.

I am extremely grateful to Holly La Due at Prestel Publishing for championing this project and shepherding it into print. Holly's experience, openness, insight, and steady hand were fundamental to making this project a rich testament to this closed chapter of design and aviation history. Thanks also to the entire Prestel staff, especially Luke Chase for handling the book's production with such brilliance, Emma Kennedy for her invaluable editorial assistance, and Angy Altamirano for her fine publicity work.

For editorial input, inspiring engagement, and fortification, I thank John Son, who helped shape the words and thoughts here. His efforts were critical to realizing a long-standing project so dear to me.

For guidance and heartfelt encouragement, I am deeply grateful to Cameron Campbell, a true friend and design visionary. Cameron demonstrates an enthusiasm, knowledge, and passion for the power of creativity that I imagine the original designers of Concorde would have appreciated.

Thank you to Helen Keyes, a design inspiration who remained a supporter of the project over many years and continents, graciously consulted on contributors to the book, and provided a gravitas that vastly elevated the tenor of the project.

To Sebastian Conran and Sir Terence Conran, a heartfelt thanks for sharing your words and memories regarding your significant design contributions to the legacy of Concorde. In the end, your vision, immeasurable experience, and design talent brought a supremely fitting last chapter to the life of Concorde. I am deeply honored and grateful to include your personal perspectives on the topic.

To Andrew Macpherson and Cindy Crawford, to see directly into the glamour of the Concorde experience through your words is a deeply appreciated, rare, and invaluable addition to this book.

I am indebted to all those who have permitted their words and images to be reproduced here. Special thanks are due to photographers François Robert, Liza Rosales, Phoebe Solomon and Christopher Wray-McMann. Their collective eye helped bring this story to life. Thank you to Wolfgang Tillmans for being one of the first to show Concorde as an object of fine art. And to Tevi Schwartz, whose magical work in image retouching helped us get to perfect every time.

Most importantly, I wish to thank the worldwide community of Concorde supporters. From the ten thousand spectators who came to Heathrow to watch the last Concorde touchdown, to the fellow collectors and the followers on Instagram and online groups, you demonstrate that the dream of innovation, of the future, of the advancement of humanity through creativity, still remains aloft fifteen years after the last Concorde landed, and hopefully far into the future.

Thank you,
Lawrence Azerrad

NOTES AND IMAGE CREDITS

NOTES:

[1] Wolfgang Tillmans, *Concorde* (1997; Cologne: Walther König, 2017).

[2] David Kamp, "Hooked on Supersonics," *Vanity Fair* (October 2003), www.vanityfair.com/news/2003/10/end-of-the-concorde-jets.

[3] "The Wright brothers' first aircraft was unstable. It was controllable (just), thanks to the slowness of the unstable pitching." Christopher Orlebar, *The Concorde Story* (London: Reed Books, 1986), 117.

[4] Emma Green, "Innovation: The History of a Buzzword," *The Atlantic,* June 20, 2013.

[5] Peter Gössel and Gabriele Leuthäuser, *Architecture in the Twentieth Century* (Cologne: Taschen, 2005), 250.

[6] The first American supersonic transport project, Boeing 2707, was canceled in 1971 after it was deemed too costly. The Soviet Tupolev Tu-144 passenger fleet was grounded in 1978 due to safety concerns.

[7] Peter Gillman, "Supersonic Bust: The Story of the Concorde," *The Atlantic* 239, no. 1 (January 1977): 72–81.

[8] Kamp, "Hooked on Supersonics."

[9] Larry Gelbart, "The Future Is Past," *New York Times*, April 26, 2003.

[10] Kamp, "Hooked on Supersonics."

[11] Gregory Votolato, *Transport Design: A Travel History* (Islington, UK: Reaktion Books, 2007), 211.

[12] Orlebar, *The Concorde Story*, 147.

[13] John Hutchinson, "Flight Fantastic: The Supersonic Age," www.youtube.com/watch?v=bpGoHx-A2gkA. Hutchinson is a former Concorde pilot.

[14] "Concorde: The Final Flight (Video #1)," www.youtube.com/watch?v=yEmzr-jW7aM.

[15] Suzanne Slesin, "New Look for a Fast Plane," *New York Times*, January 27, 1994.

[16] "Terence Conran: Flights of Fancy," January 21, 2011, www.nowness.com/story/terence-conran-flights-of-fancy.

IMAGE CREDITS:

Unless otherwise indicated, all images are from the collection of the author.

Photos by François Robert, Liza Rosales, Phoebe Solomon and Christopher Wray-McCann

Additional credits and sources are as follows:

Page 8: Photo Martyn Hayhow, Courtesy AFP/Getty Images

Page 20: Press Association Images/PA Archive/PA Images

Pages 58–59: Photo: Keystone-France, Courtesy Gamma-Keystone/Getty Images

Page 60: Photo: Chris Ware, Courtesy Hulton Archive/Getty Images

Page 61: Photo: Central Press, Courtesy Hulton Archive/Getty Images

Pages 64–65(L), 85(R), 152: © Musée Air France

Pages 82, 94, 95: © Chris Barham/ANL/REX/Shutterstock

Page 84: Courtesy GRANGER

Page 93: © Nick Rogers/ANL/REX/Shutterstock

Pages 96–97, 99, 180–181: PA/PA Archive/PA Images

Page 98(B): © Paul Fievez/ANL/REX/Shutterstock

Pages 100–101: © Bill Howard/ANL/REX/Shutterstock

Page 109: Photo: Jim Sugar, Courtesy Corbis Historical/Getty Images

Page 112: © Reginald Davis/REX/Shutterstock

Pages 126, 132, 140: © and courtesy the Adrian Meredith Concorde Collection

Pages 131, 159: Photo: Etienne De Malglaive, Courtesy Gamma-Rapho/Getty Images

Page 135: © Mike Hollist/ANL/REX/Shutterstock

Page 138: © John Voos/The Independent/REX/Shutterstock

Page 149: Photo: Jack Garofalo, Courtesy Paris Match Archive/Getty Images

Pages 151, 153: © UMDADC/REX/Shutterstock

Page 164: Courtesy Factorydesign

Page 165: Courtesy Bonhams

Page 170(L): © REX/Shutterstock

Page 171: Stefan Rousseau/PA Archive/PA Images

Pages 174, 175: © Geraint Lewis / Alamy Stock Photo

Pages 182–183: FABIANO/SIPA

The author on board British Airways Concorde, July 8, 2003.

About the Author

Lawrence Azerrad is a Grammy Award–winning, Los Angeles–based graphic designer and creative director. Azerrad founded LADdesign, a graphic design studio focusing on the intersections of music, education, cultural initiatives, and branding.

Since 2001 LADdesign has created graphic design and comprehensive visual identity systems for clients such as Sting, Universal Music Group, UC San Diego, USC Roski School of Art and Design, Blue Note Records, Silversun Pickups, Esperanza Spalding, Wilco, Skirball Cultural Center, The Beach Boys, WeTransfer, and UCLA.

Azerrad is a producer and creative director of *The Voyager Golden Record: 40th Anniversary Edition.* Azerrad is the chair for AIGA's Design + Music program, a national initiative to explore how design thinking can make a positive impact on the music industry and American culture at large through innovation and creative excellence.

Azerrad has spoken on design and inspiration at TEDxUCLA and the Amazon Conflux 2017 Conference.

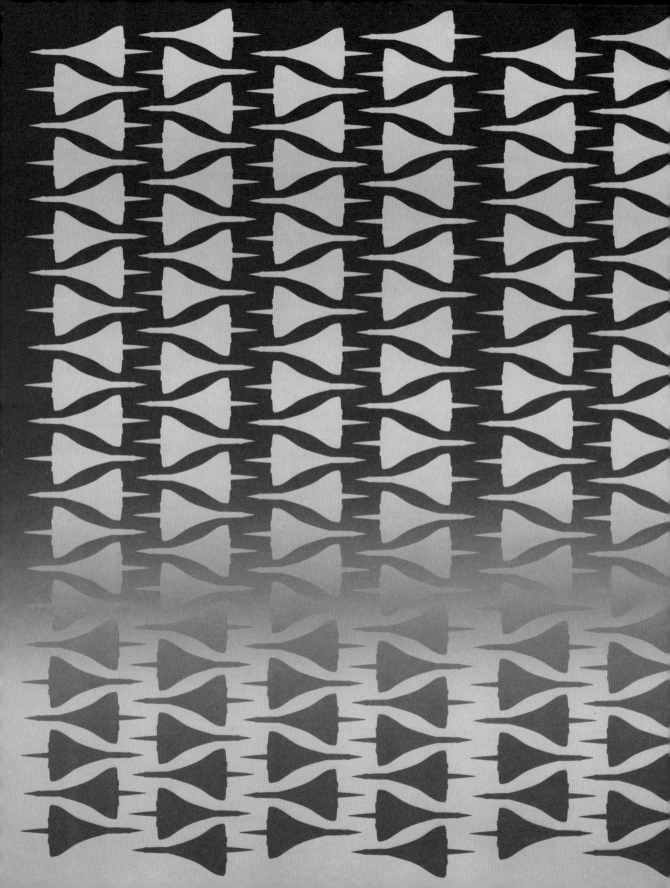